UNITED ARAB EMIRATES

Text & Photos

CHRISTINE OSBORNE

Author: Christine Osborne
Title: Old Gulf Coast Days: United Arab Emirates
ISBN: 97809923240-6-3

Subjects: United Arab Emirates
          Pictorial works
          Abu Dhabi
          Dubai
          Sharjah
          Ajman
          Umm al-Qawain
          Ras al-Khaimah
          Fujairah

Cover: Waterfront in central Ajman, 1974: Christine Osborne
Page 5: Landscape in Dubai hinterland: Tim Gurney OBE.

A catalogue reference for this book is available from
The National Library of Australia

While researching my book on the Arab States of the Gulf, I received a letter from my mother addressed: Christine Osborne c/- InterContinental Hotel, Dubai, Trucial States. The address was not surprising since at her age, *Trucial States* was the only name she had known. And that the letter found me was because the fledgling nation of seven Arab states possessed only five hotels between them at the time.

My association with the United Arab Emirates began in 1974 when I stopped en route home for Christmas in Australia. I had never set foot in the Arabian Peninsula and as my flight from London neared Dubai, oil flares winked up from the dark waters of the Gulf. Were they telling me something?

In the morning, I beheld a sight that took my breath away. Some 80-90 dhows, flying flags from Iran, Pakistan, Kenya and Zanzibar, were discharging cargo along the banks of Dubai creek. It was a scene from the 'Arabian Nights' and in that moment, I resolved to return and write a book about the region.

In 1975 I flew into Abu Dhabi, the UAE island capital, to begin the task.

It was groundbreaking work. There were no maps, but then there were no street names. I went about barefoot as my shoes kept filling up with sand. Interviews with officials were often arranged late at night. On one occasion, with nowhere to stay in the eastern emirate of Fujairah, I slept under the desert stars.

While Dubai has developed into an international tourist resort, the real miracle of oil wealth is seen in Abu Dhabi's vast afforestation schemes initiated by its ruler and the first UAE president, HH Sheikh Zayed bin Sultan al-Nahyan (1918-2004).

That first visit I travelled into town on an airport road lined with yellow sand dunes. On my last visit in the 1990s, I drove into a highrise city through lush green forests. Over the years I witnessed extraordinary changes as the emirates caught up with the 20th century, but the most interesting period was the early days of development in the 1970s.

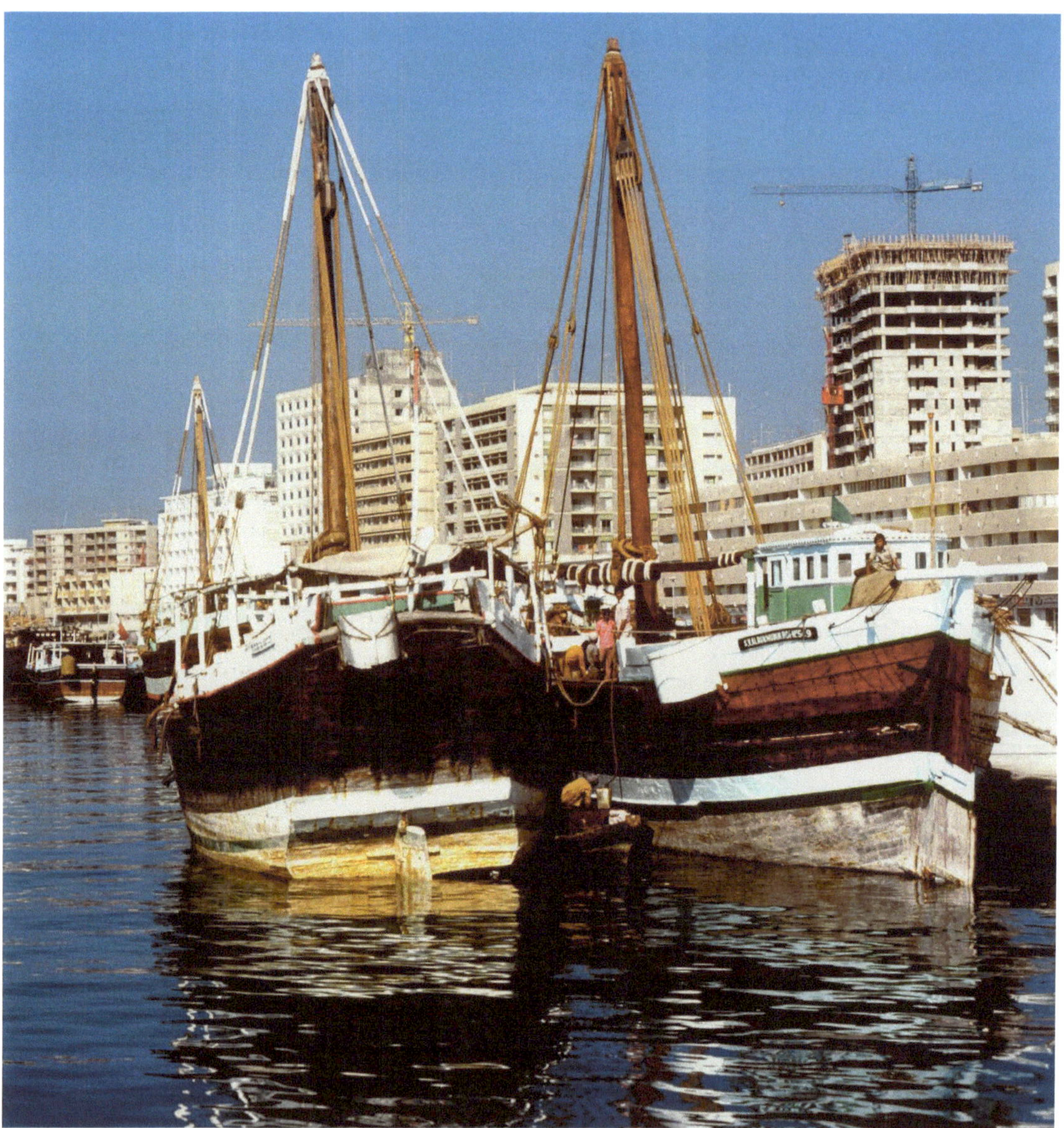

The United Arab Emirates is a federation of seven sheikhdoms, formerly known as the Trucial States, established in 1971 when Britain annulled the Maritime Treaty of Peace in Perpetuity agreement of 1853. Abu Dhabi, the capital and largest emirate accounts for 87 per cent of the UAE's total area of 83,600 sq km, or roughly the size of Austria. Other members are Dubai, Sharjah, Ajman, Umm al-Qawain, Ras al-Khaimah and Fujairah. All border the Arabian Gulf with the exception of Fujairah which lies on the Gulf of Oman. Sharjah also has a small enclave on this coastline. The benefits of a united front following the departure of their British guarantor were obvious. But it was essential people set aside old feuds largely centred on guarding their territory against tribal incursions. More than a score of different tribes inhabit the coastal band and interior of the UAE. Prominent are the Bani Yas in Abu Dhabi; the al Bu-Falasah, a branch of the Bani Yas in Dubai; the al-Na'im in Ajman; the al-Ali in Umm al-Qawain; the Sharqiyin in Fujairah; the al-Qasimi in Sharjah and the Qawasim in Ras al-Khaimah whose big seafaring dhows harassing British ships led to the aforementioned peace treaty. Involving the six emirs in decision making under the guidance of the first UAE president, Sheikh Zayed bin Sultan al-Nahyan of Abu Dhabi, was crucial to the union's success. Several high profile rulers were appointed to the federal council. Other representatives from each emirate were given ministerial posts. Among many early projects was the provision of free land and housing to draw the Bedouin into urban settlements. Prior to the discovery of oil, most people in the Trucial States had lived at subsistence level, the men migrating between inland oases for the annual date harvest and to the coast for employment as fishermen and pearl divers. Real development—roads, electricity, hospitals and schools—did not start in earnest until the 1980s, since when the UAE has progressed at a pace unimaginable in the 'Old Gulf Coast' days. But while westernisation in all it's manifestations was inevitable, Emirati culture remains rooted in a combination of Bedouin traditions and the teachings of Islam. The national symbol of the UAE is the falcon which appears on the coat of arms.

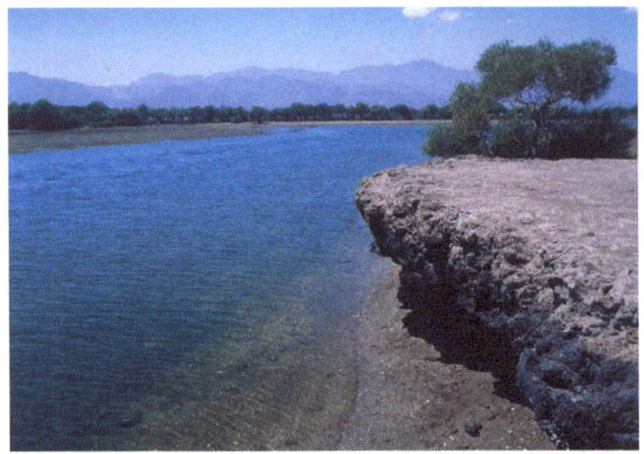

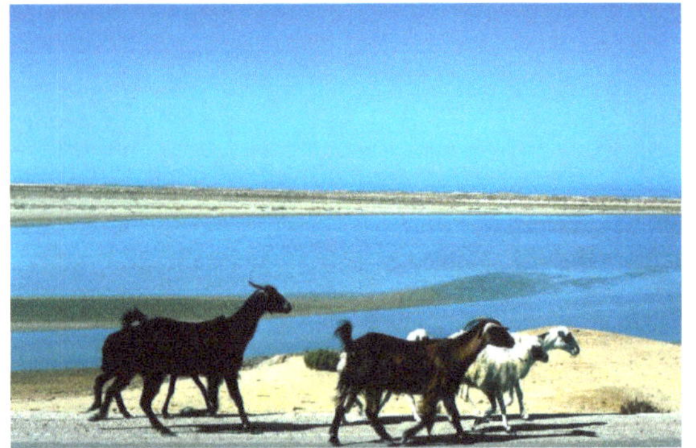

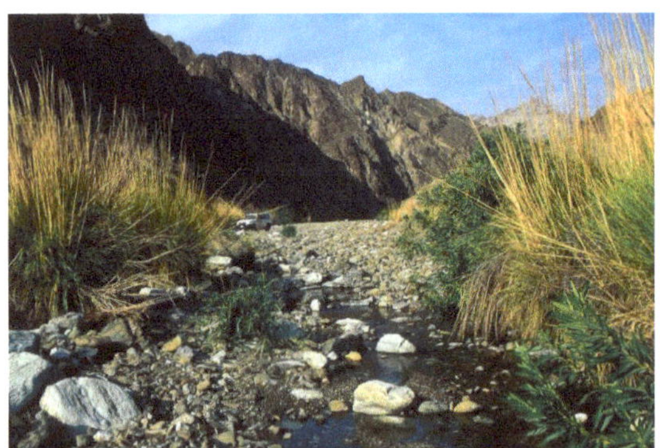

Sandy beaches interspersed with mud flats or *sabkha*, characterise the UAE coastline. Inland is largely desert rising in massive wind blown dunes surrounding Abu Dhabi's Liwa oasis. While deserts are synonymous with Arabia, the Hajar Mountains bordering Oman define the northern emirates of Ras al-Khaimah and Fujairah. The highest peak—2,500m in Ras al-Khaimah—may experience snow. Otherwise the UAE is hot and dry and very humid on the coast. Rainfall, once as little as 120mm, has increased due to vast afforestation schemes Native vegetation is limited to arid zone grasses and trees such as the *ghaf* which can send a tap root down 30m to reach water. The dwarf tamarisk and *babul*, or Arabian gum tree are other indigenous species. Date palms flourish around underground springs.

Top: Khor Kalba Nature Park in East Sharjah is known for birdlife.

Centre: lagoons and *sabkha* mud flats border the coastline of Umm al-Qawain.

Lower: native vegetation lines a stream in the eastern Emirate of Fujairah.

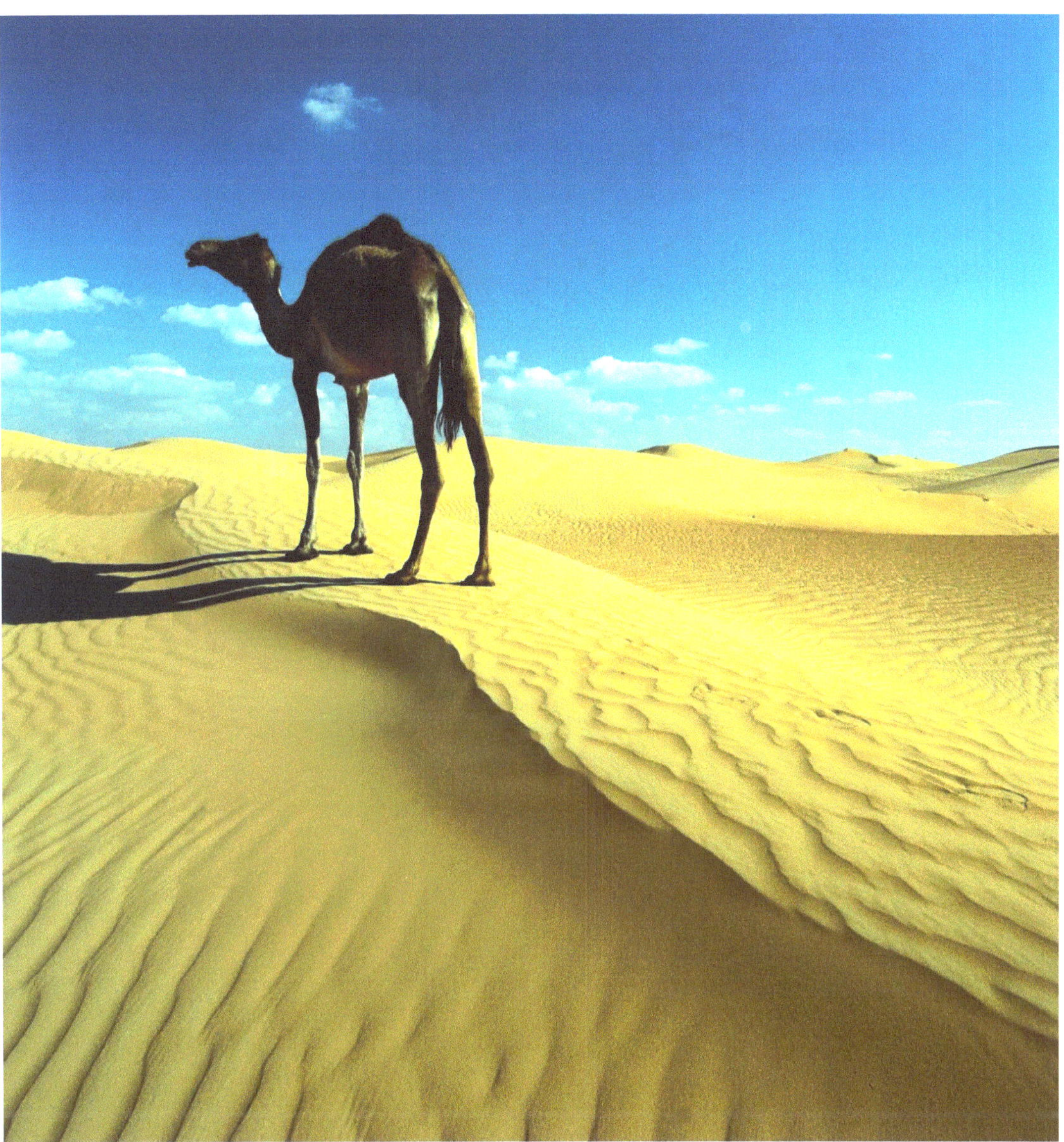

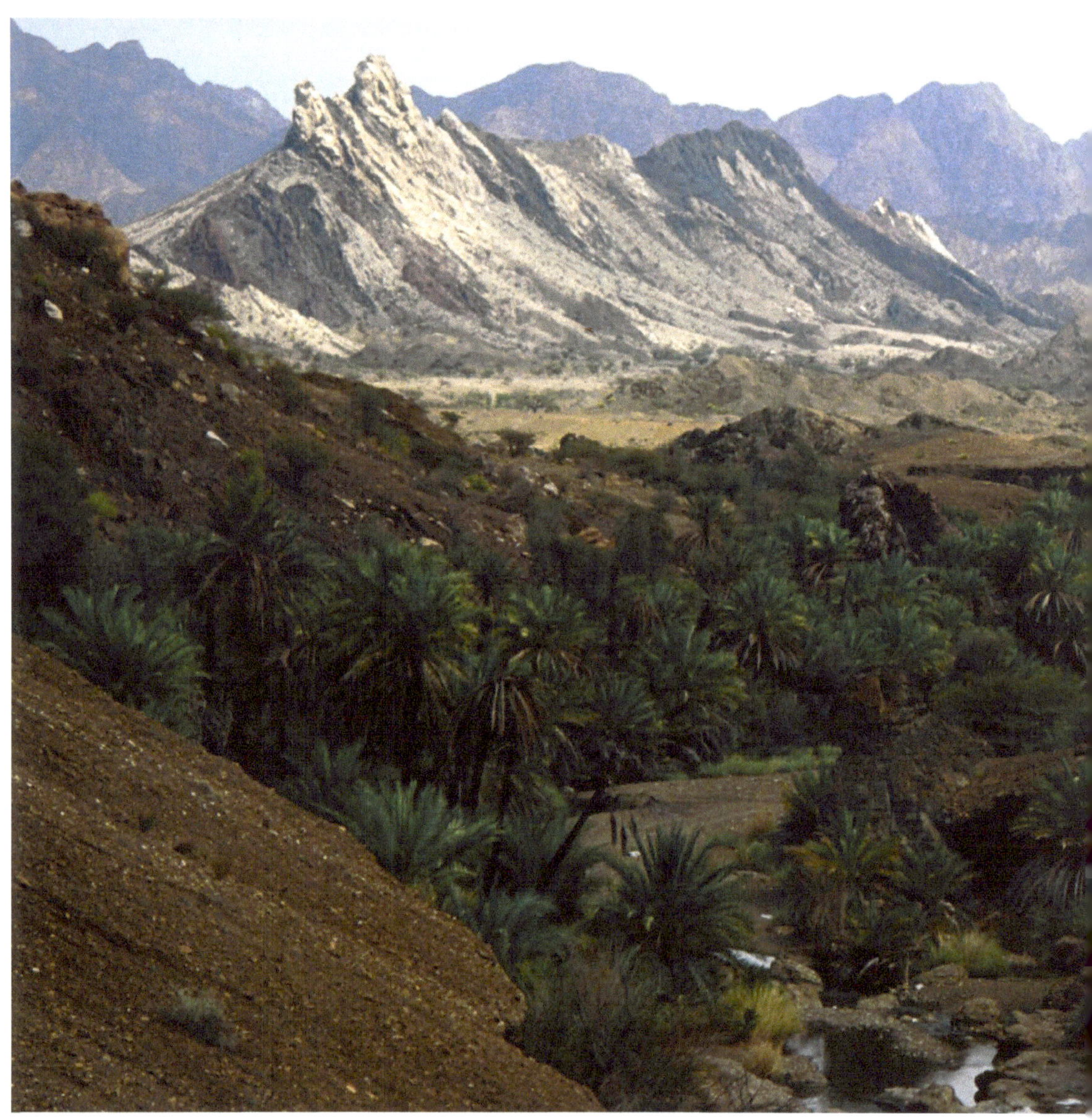

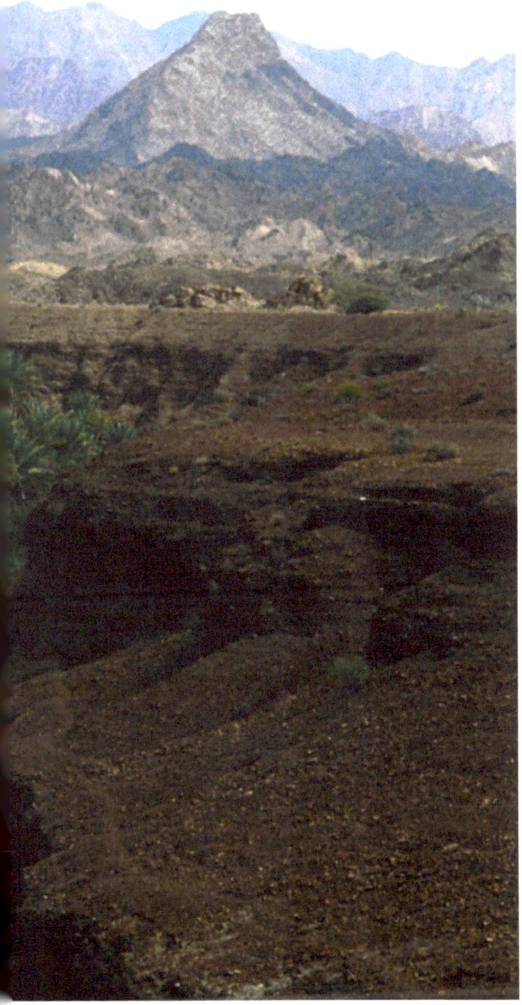

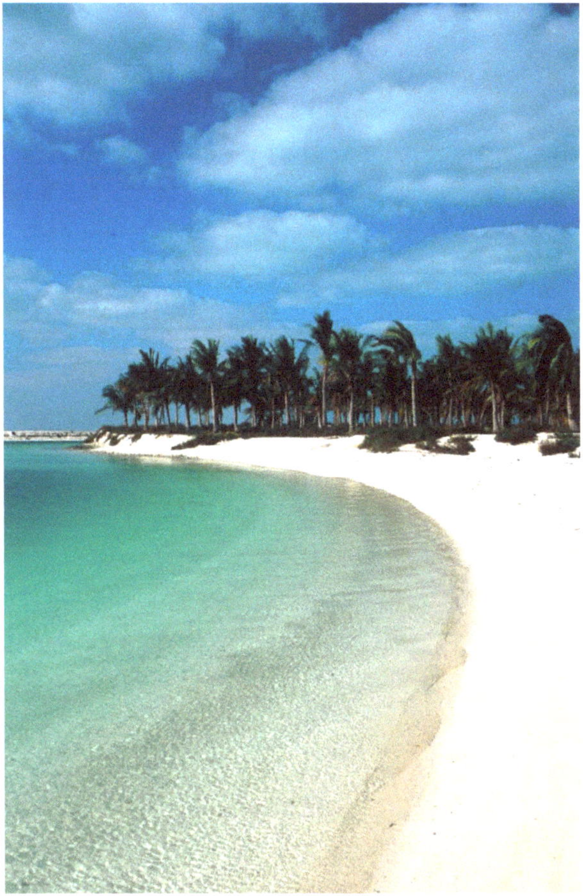

This page: white sand beach on Abu Dhabi was created using land reclaimed from the sea.

Opposite: view of Wadi Hatta in eastern Dubai with the Hajar Mountains in the distance.

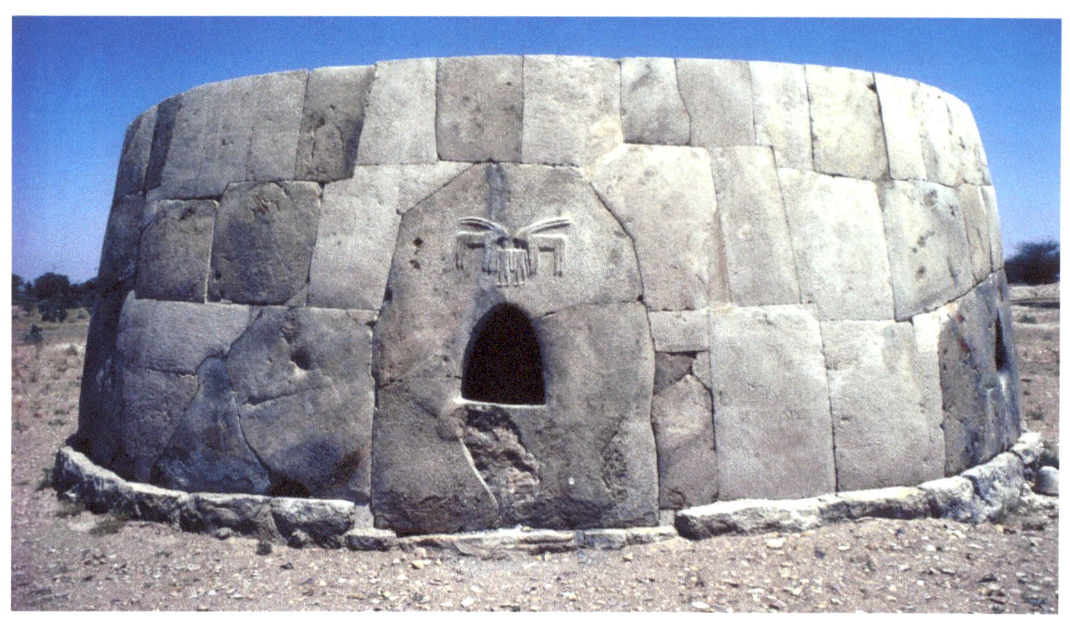

The UAE was only conceived in the twentieth century, but its history stretches back 7,000 years. Archaeological excavation had barely begun in the 1970s and what was then known about its past has since multiplied threefold. Early finds on Umm an-Nar island in Abu Dhabi include fifty stone burial cairns of citizens who lived during the Bronze Age (2500-2000 BCE). Among cultural sites around the inland town of al-Ain is the large tomb at al-Hili linked to the Umm an-Nar period. A bas relief depicts Arabian oryx and a couple holding hands. Flint stone tools and arrow heads and pieces of Ubaid Age (5000-4000 BCE) pottery have been discovered in Umm al-Qawain and Ras al-Khaimah. Shell and dugong bone middens have been found elsewhere. Clearly much still remains hidden beneath the sands but both from the mainland and off-shore islands, artefacts are gradually being unearthed that confirm the ancient inhabitants of the lower Gulf were trading with their contemporaries in southern Mesopotamia.

Opposite right: mid-19th century watch tower in Ras al-Khaimah.

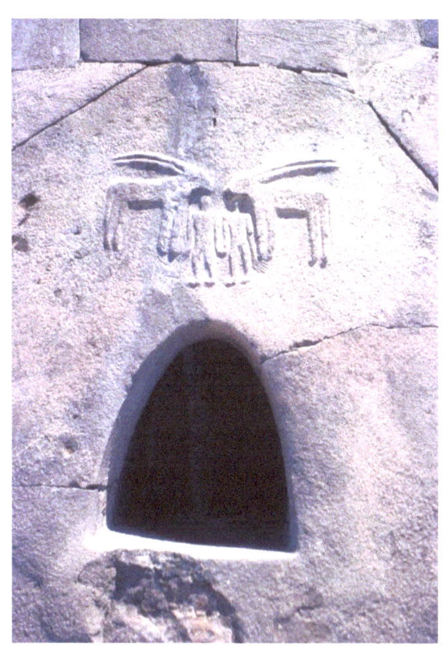

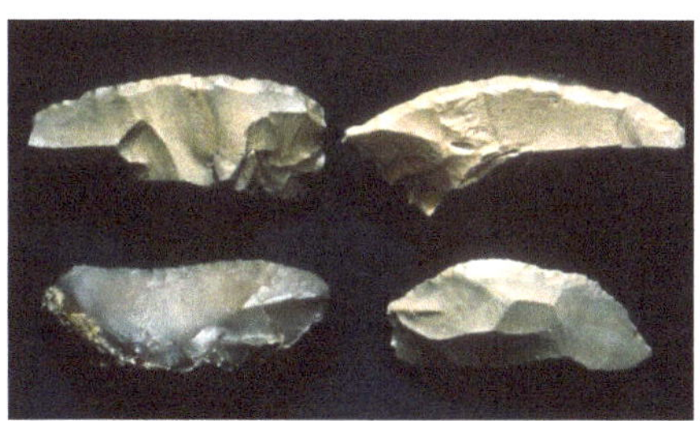

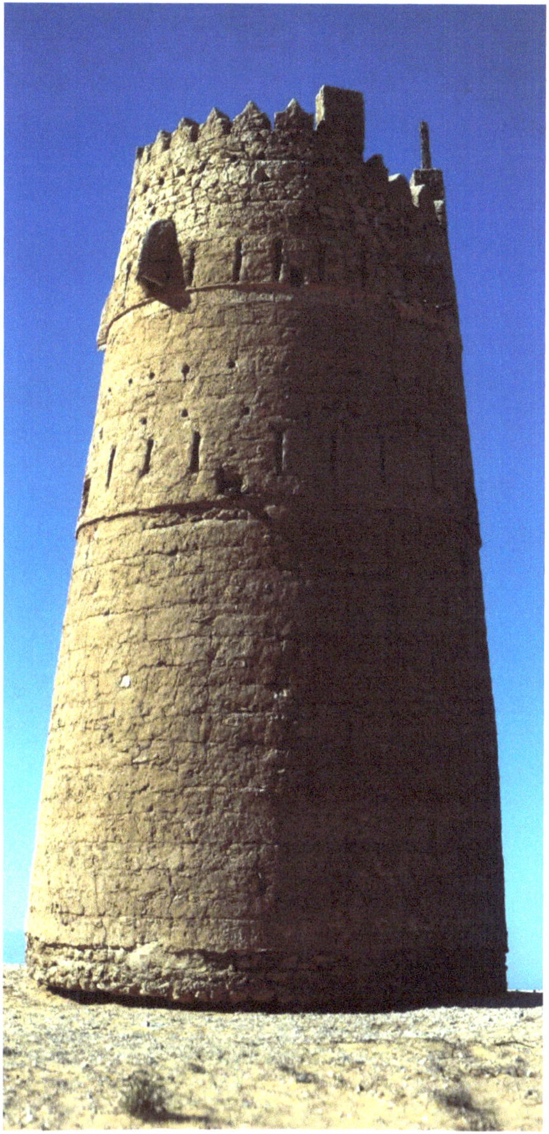

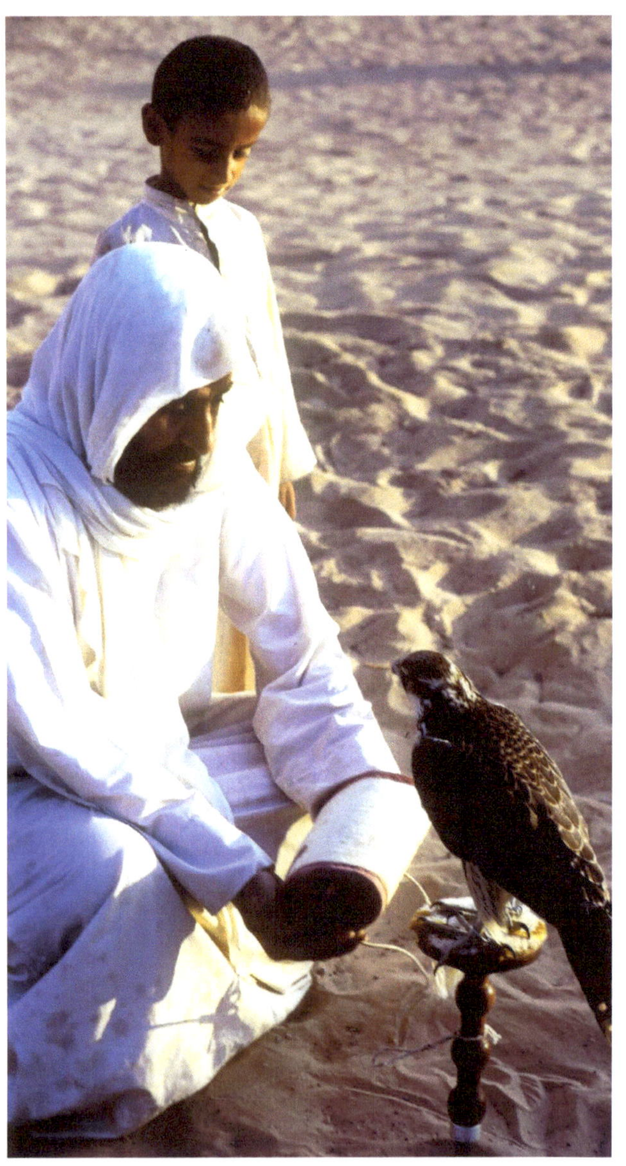

Living in the desert hinterland the Bedouin developed a philosophy suited to their means of survival in the inhospitable environment. Cherishing freedom above comforts, they owned only what mobility allowed. Most kept several camels to travel to the coast for supplies, often traded by barter. There were no roads. The journey from Buraimi oasis to Abu Dhabi, took 5-7 days. Some may have owned a radio, but for the most part news was passed by word of mouth.

Falconry was the main leisure pursuit. The quarry *houbara* bustard made a welcome change from rice and dates.

This page: a Bedouin trains his falcon to sit upright on a perch.

Opposite top: a Bedouin leads a stray camel back to his campsite.

Lower: most tents had only three poles. Pitched against Jebel Hafit in Abu Dhabi, this tent belonged to a prominent tribal sheikh.

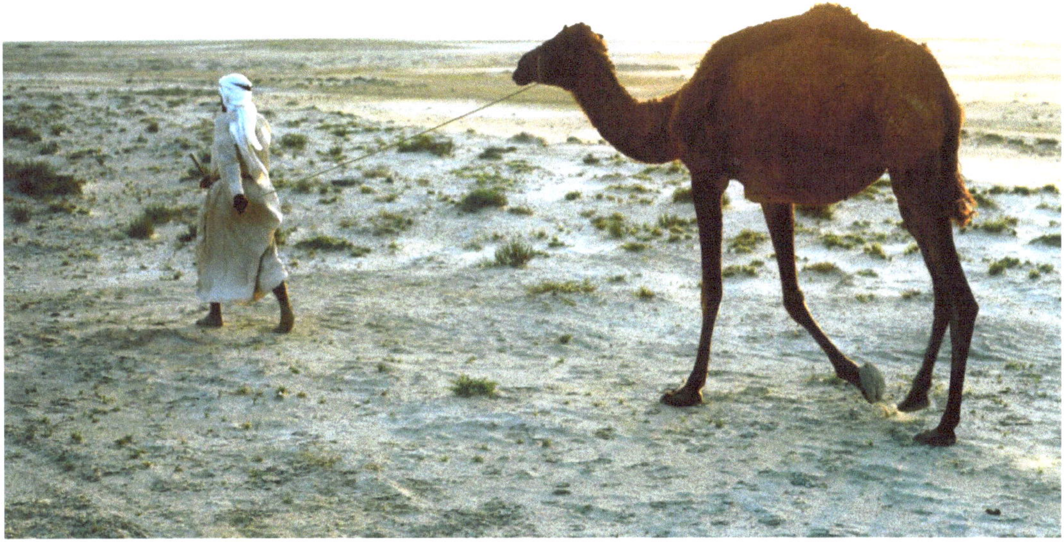

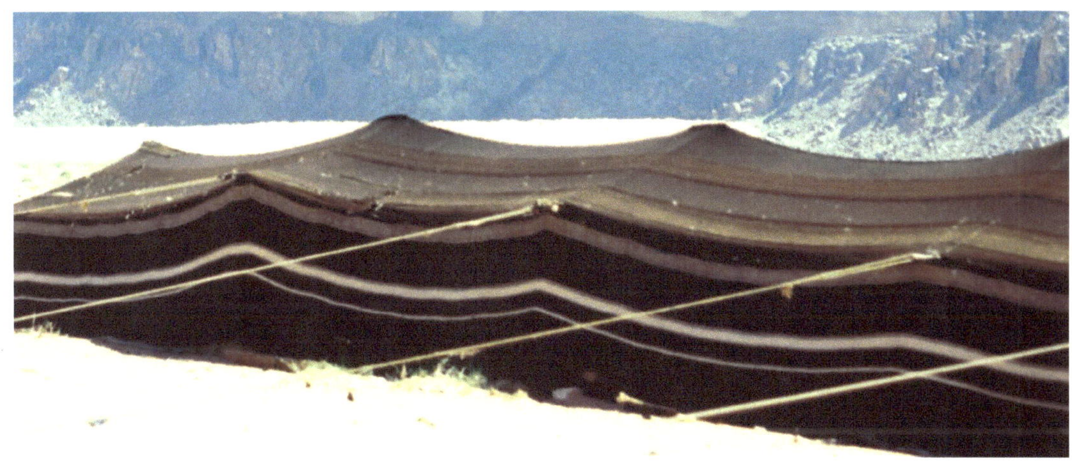

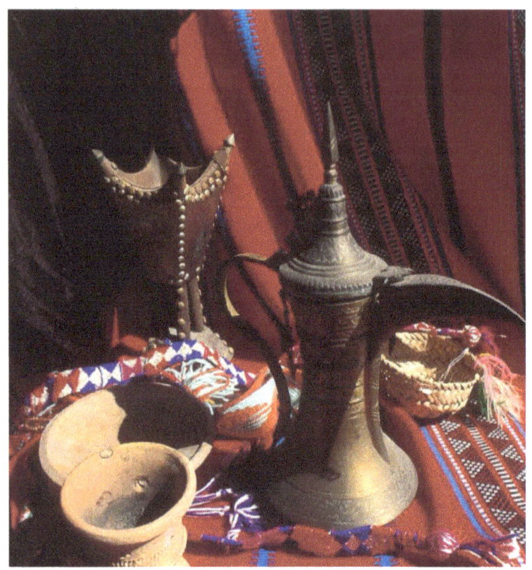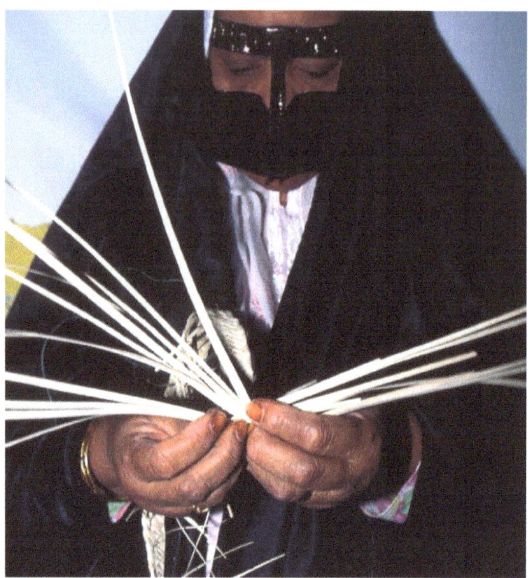

Hospitality is a traditional custom among the Bedouin. Coffee and dates were always offered to any visitor to their campsite. The *dallah,* or Arabic coffee-pot with its peaked spout, is as much a symbol of the UAE as the falcon. Life was tedious for Bedouin women left to spend all day around the tent. Weaving from wool, goat and spun camel hair was their only creative craft: mats for sleeping on, rugs for the cold desert nights and a curtain dividing the tent in two. One side was the women's domain for cooking and sleeping, the other used for eating and entertaining by the men. Several wives as permitted by Islam was usual. The *burqa* face mask is worn by all adult women.

This page: a Bedouin woman weaving a basket from raked date palm fronds.

Opposite: a Bedouin woman making buttermilk in a goatskin bag swung from a tripod stuck in the sand outside her tent in Dubai, 1974.

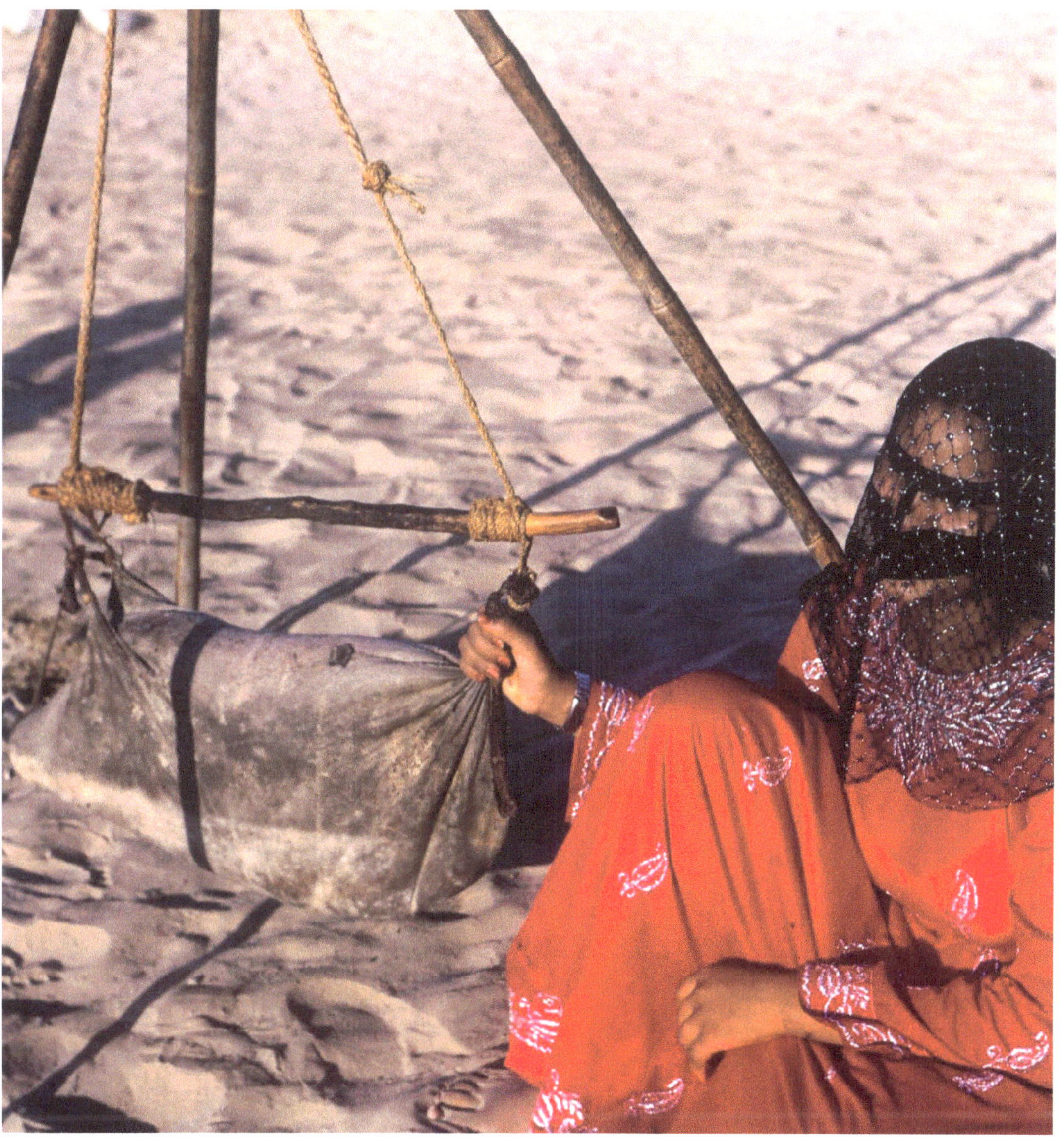

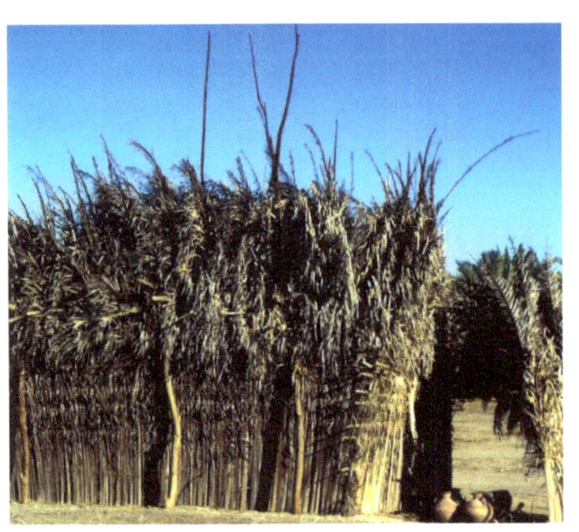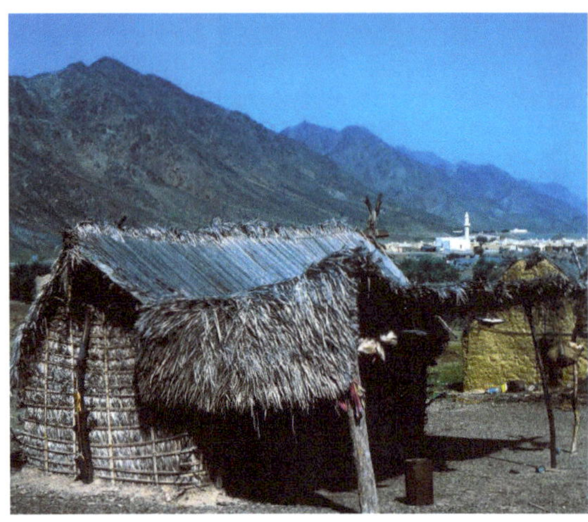

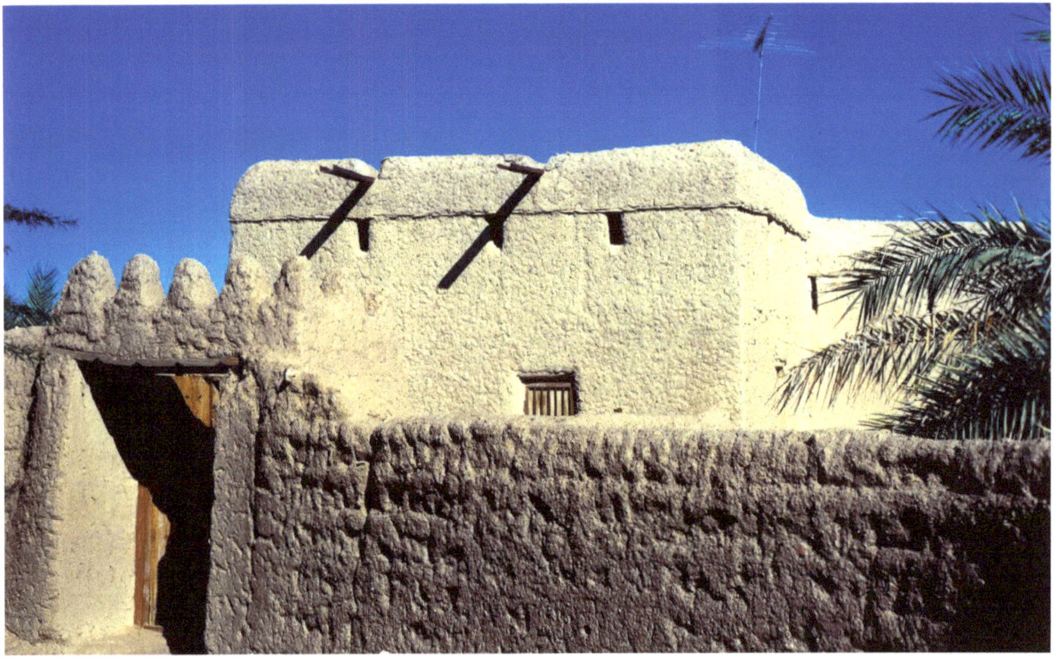

Coastal peoples in the northern emirates lived in what were known as *barastis*. Simple huts fashioned from date palm fronds lashed on a wooden frame, they allowed cooling breezes to circulate during the hot summers. Cooking, done on an open hearth, made them very fire prone. Similarly made and with palm matting roofs for shade, the old *souqs* in both Dubai and Abu Dhabi burned down during the 1960s.

Opposite top: *barastis* in Ras al-Khaimah (left) and Fujairah (right).

Lower: the owner of this traditional mud daub house, typical of the oasis town of al-Ain in Abu Dhabi was able to afford a television. He cultivated a few vegetables - eggplants and squash for sale and owned a single date palm

This page: a desert ghetto housing migrant construction workers on the Dubai-Sharjah border in 1974. The *barastis* were made from date palm fronds, mangrove poles and hessian bags. Each hut was topped with a crude wooden wind-tower.

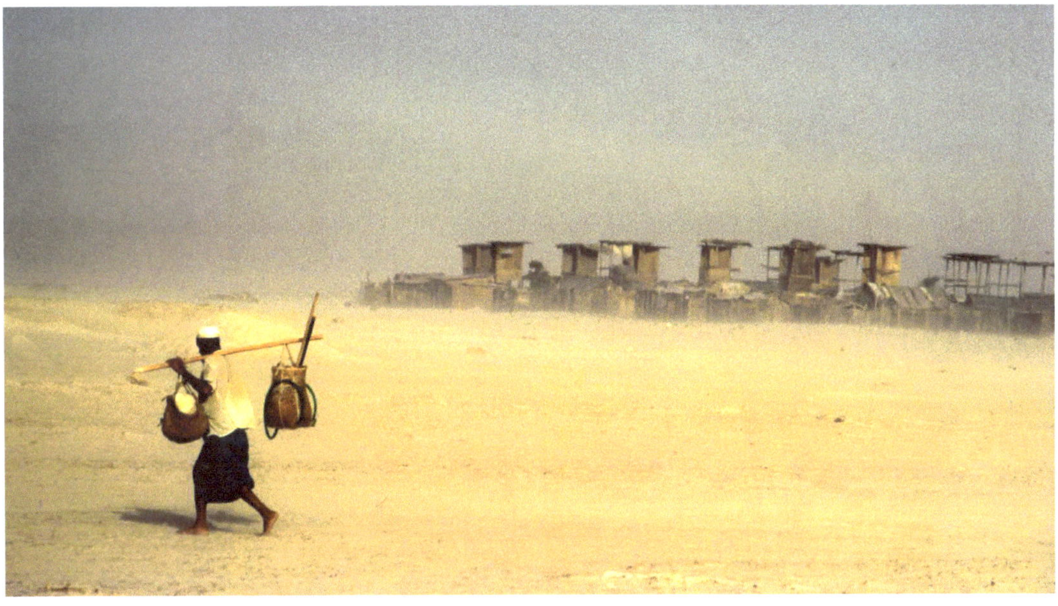

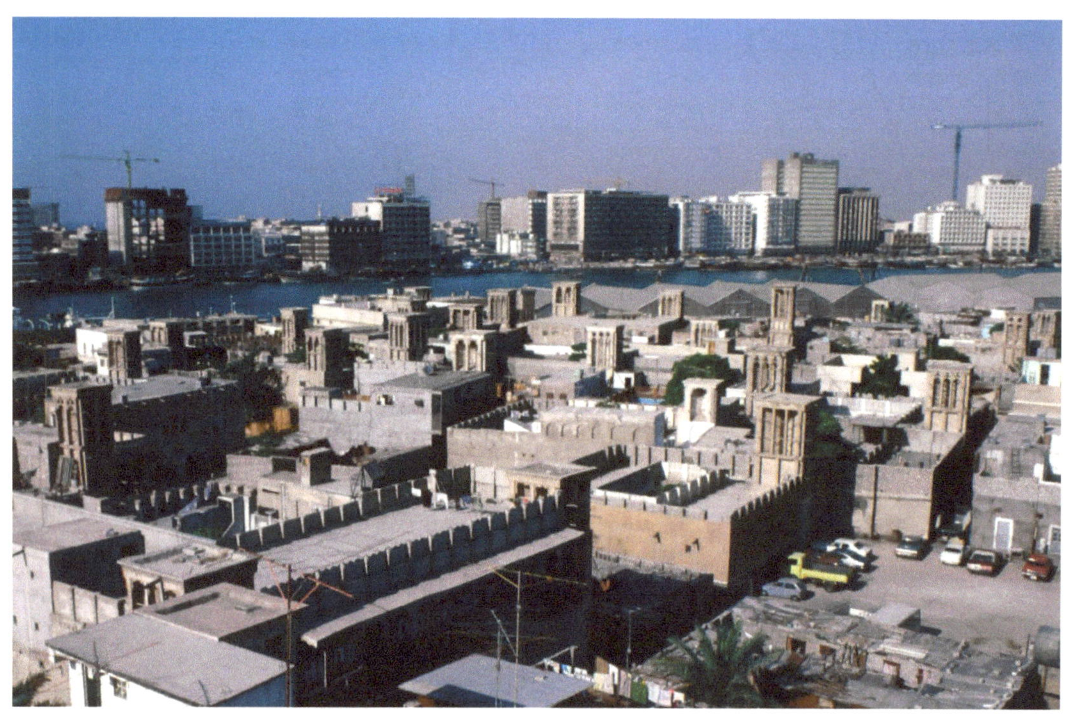

A contrast to the fragile *barastis* are the solid coral and limestone houses built by Iranian merchant families who moved to Dubai in the early 19th century to escape persecution from the Shi'a regime in Tehran. Located in the historic Bastakia quarter on the west bank of Dubai creek, they are distinguished for their carved wind-towers or *badgirs*. A simple, but effective form of air conditioning originating in Persia, the multi-sided structures can funnel down any cool air currents to the rooms below. Some houses display decorative windows (opposite).

Following pages: fishermen repairing their nets in Khor Fakkan, East Sharjah, 1975.

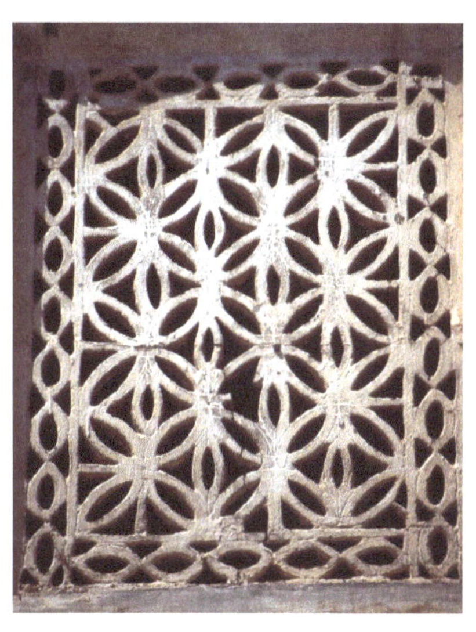

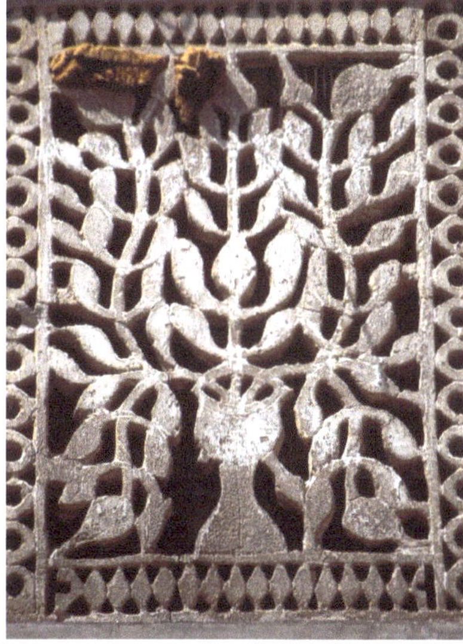

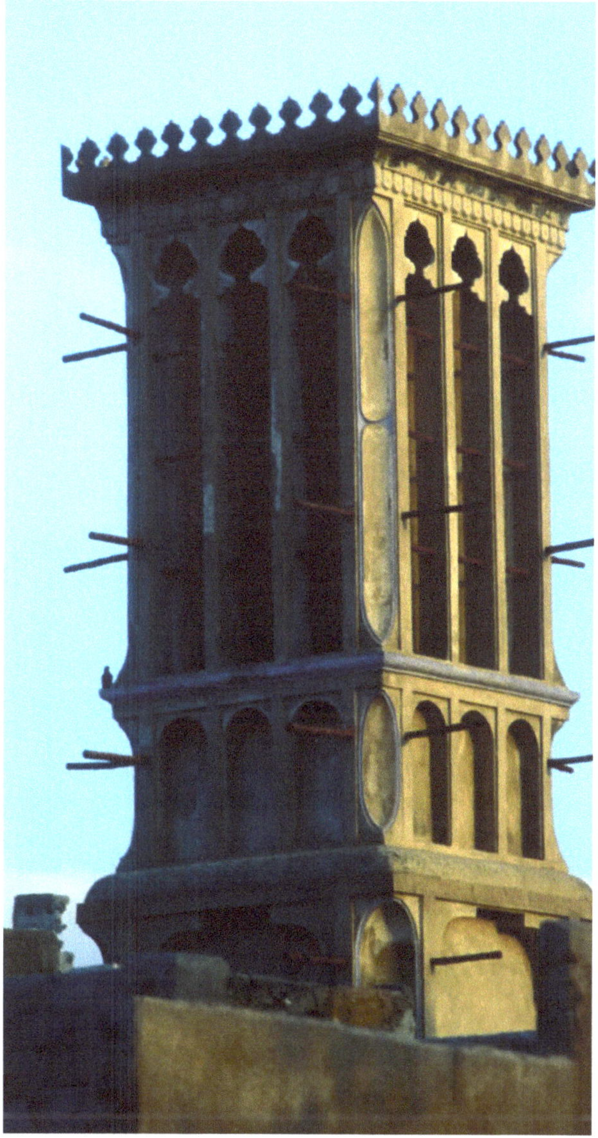

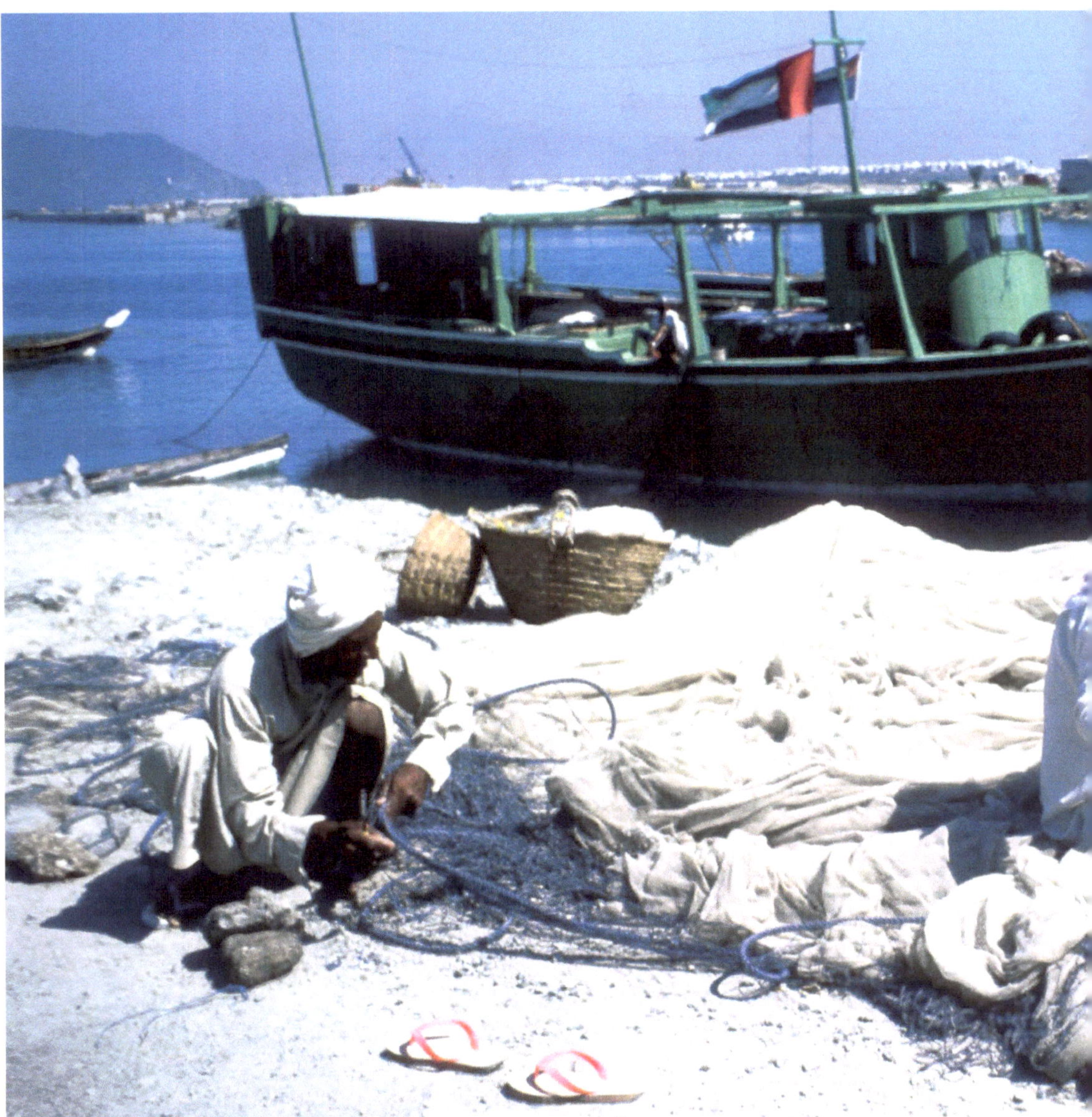

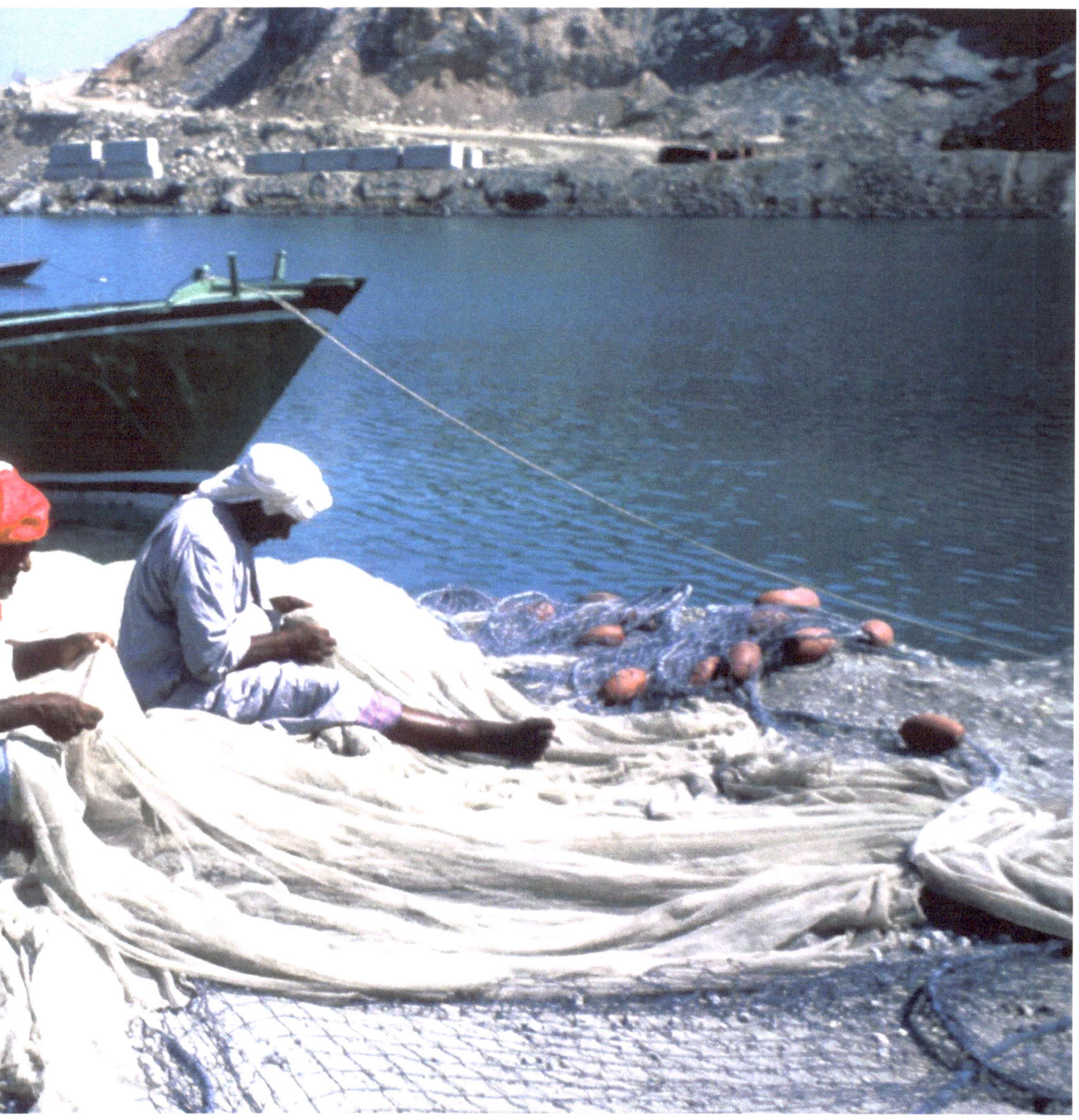

Fishing and pearling were the main activities of coastal communities in the UAE. Dubai was also very much involved in commerce on which its reputation is based.

This page: one of the last traditional tidal fish traps on the island of Abu Dhabi.

Opposite top left: weaving a wire *ghandour* fish trap in Dubai.

Opposite top right: traders weigh slabs of rock salt in Ras al-Khaimah. Crushed it was used for drying fish, a source of animal feed in the interior.

Lower: fishermen drag a haul of sardines onto the beach in Fujairah, Gulf of Oman.

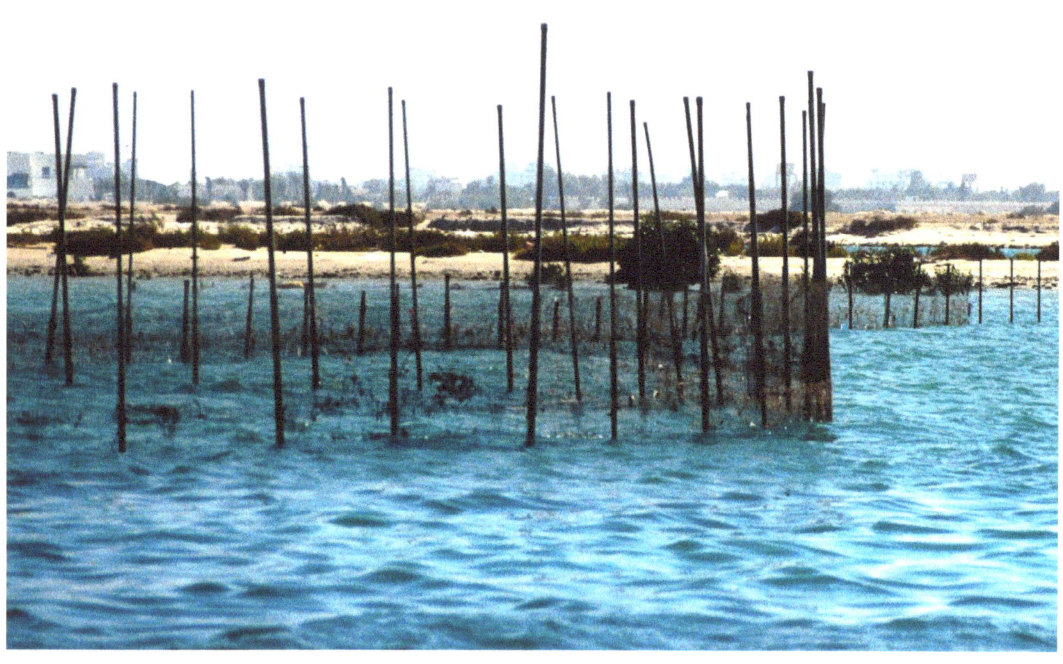

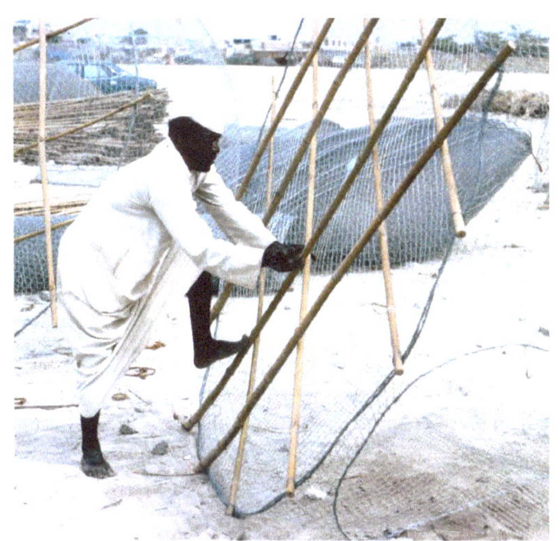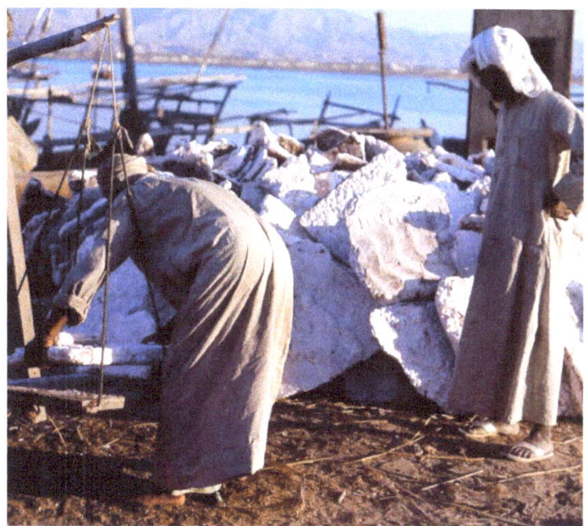

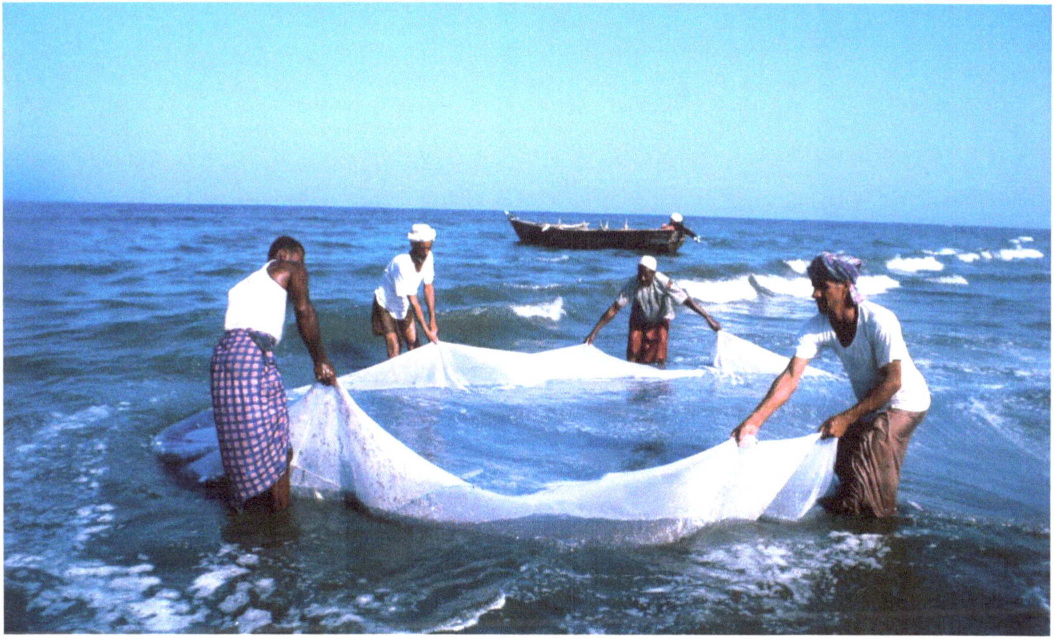

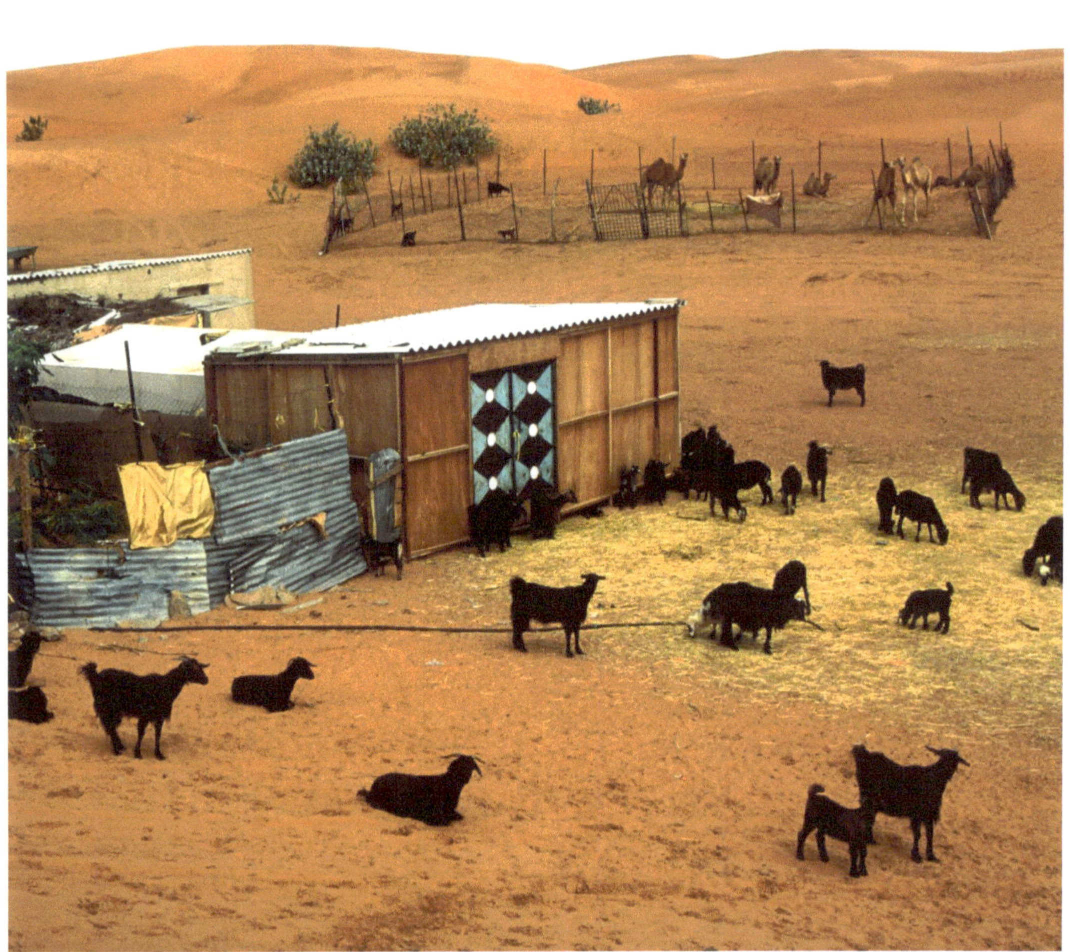

Some Emiratis owned small holdings such as this livestock farm in the Dubai hinterland.

Others lived a peripatetic existence working as fishermen and date pickers according to the seasons. Two of the largest date oases are Liwa and Buraimi in inland Abu Dhabi (the latter is shared with Oman).

This page top: a tobacco farm in the eastern emirate of Fujairah.

Lower: a date palm grove sustained on underground spring water in Ras al-Khaimah.

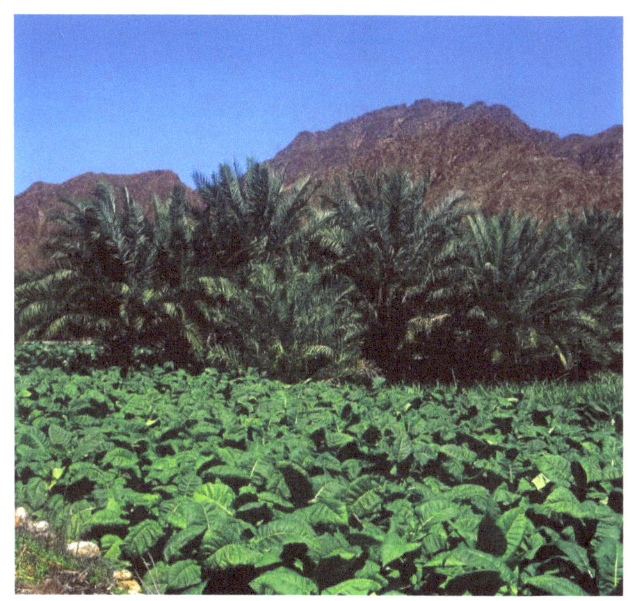

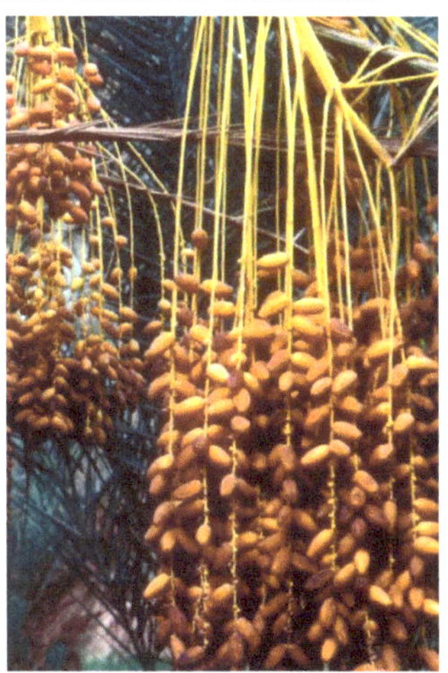

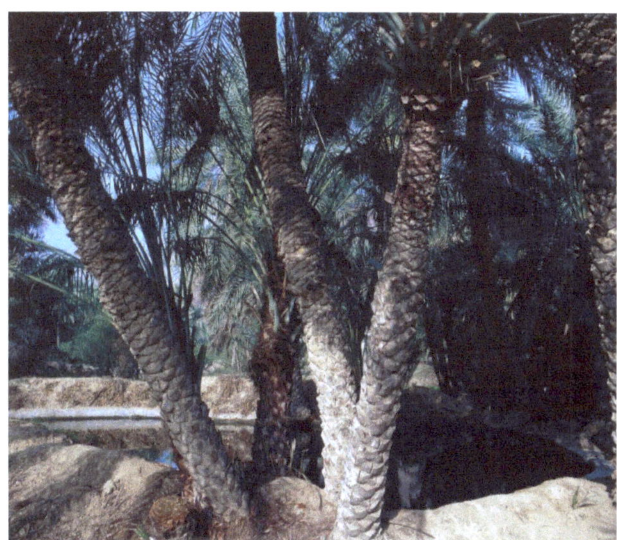

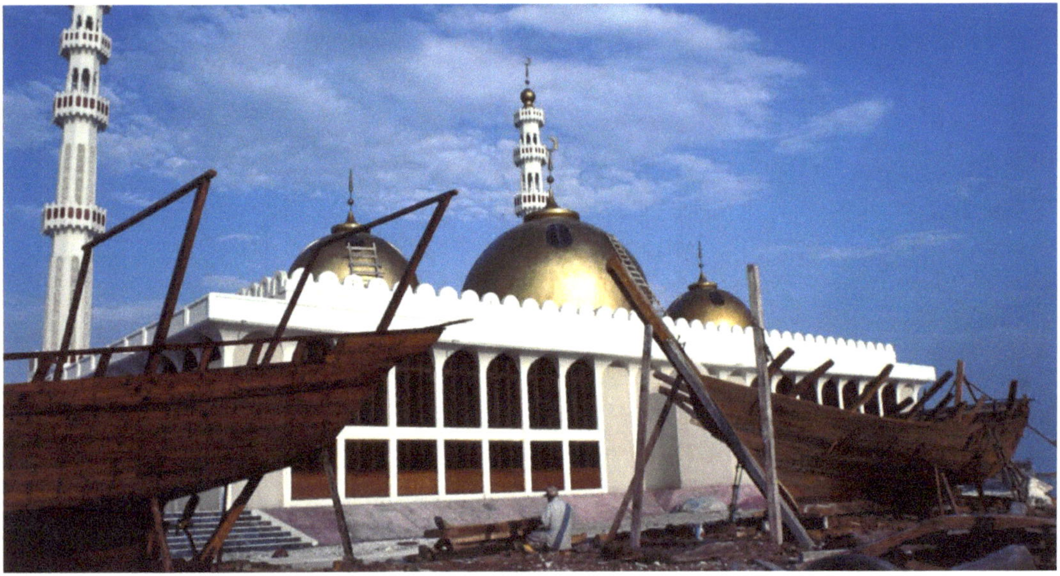

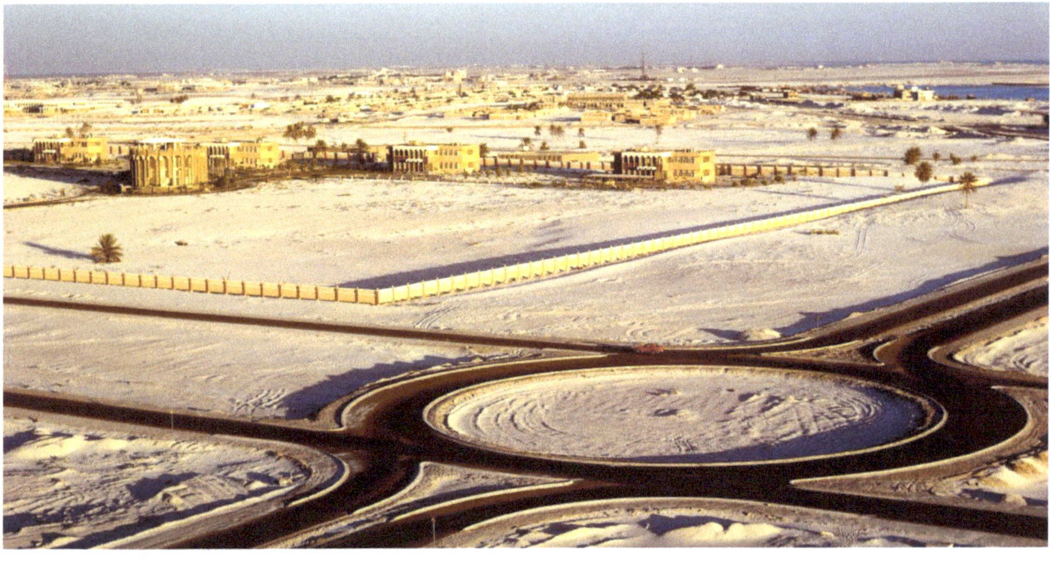

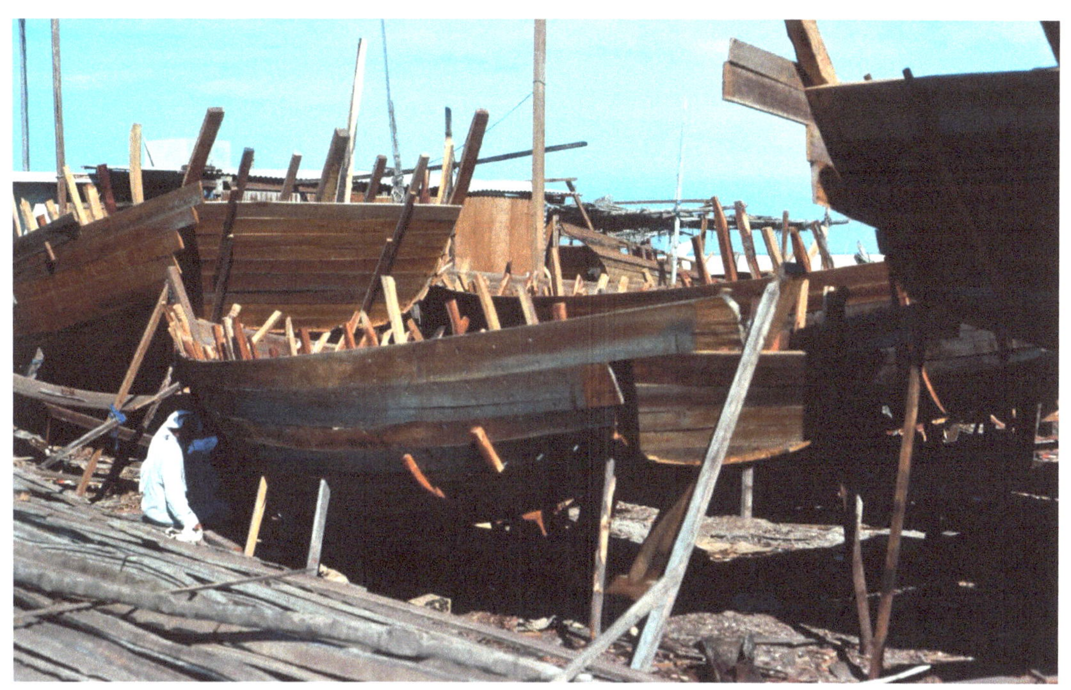

Dhow building employed a few skilled craftsmen in the small emirate of Ajman from at least the 1800s. Dhows are still built today, but workmen use modern tools and the hull may be cement or fibre glass. **This page:** Ajman dhow yard in 1974.

Opposite top: Abu Dhabi had a small dhow yard located in al-Bateen district.
Lower: al-Bateen in 1978. The dhow yard is just visible top right corner.

Following pages: big Kuwaiti *boums* moored on Dubai creek were used for running gold between Dubai and Bombay. Powered by 240-300 hp motors, often Rolls Royce engines removed from tanks left by the British in Sharjah, they could easily outrun Indian coastal patrols. The trade was legal from Dubai's point of view.

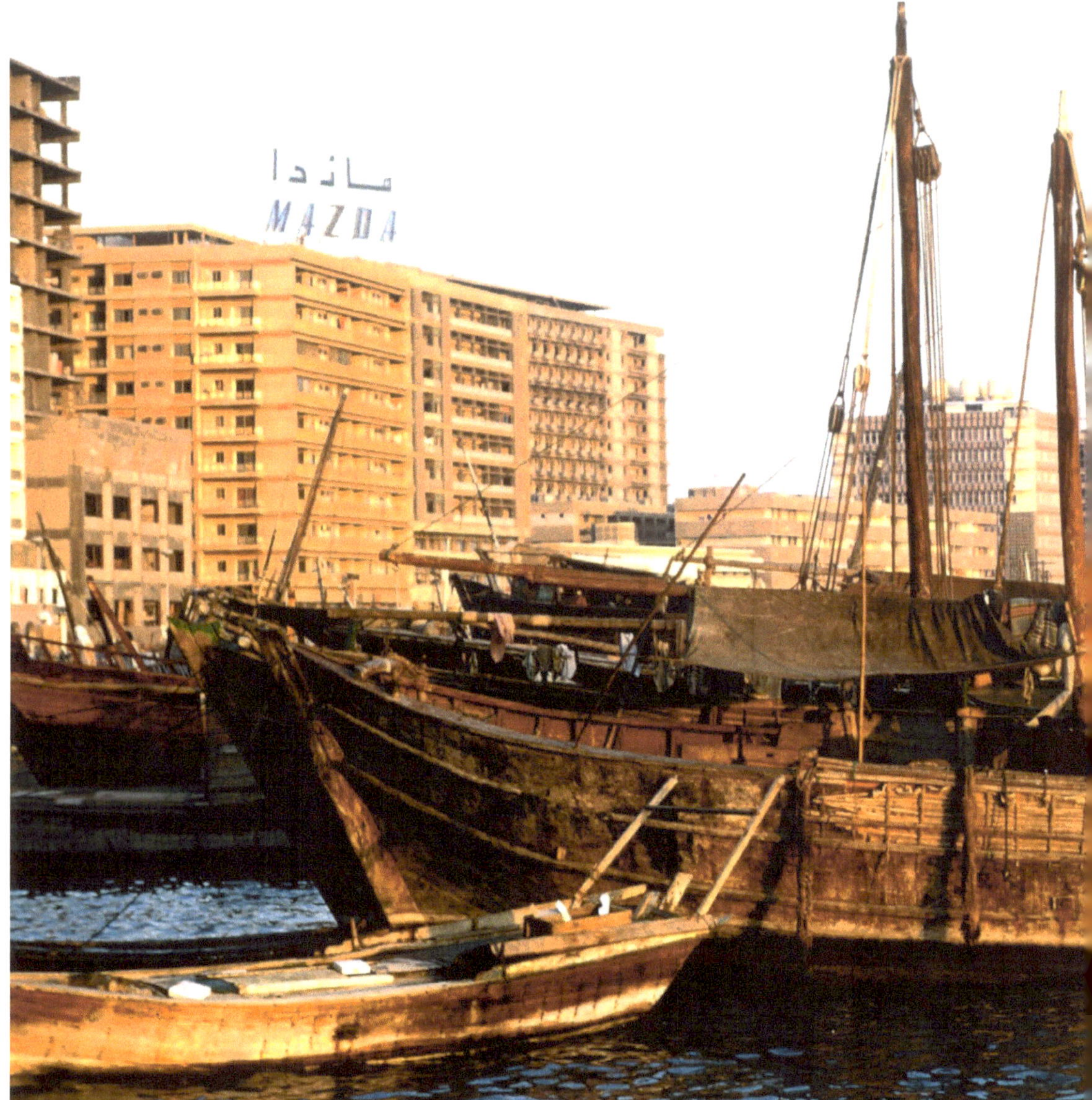
ماذا
MAZDA

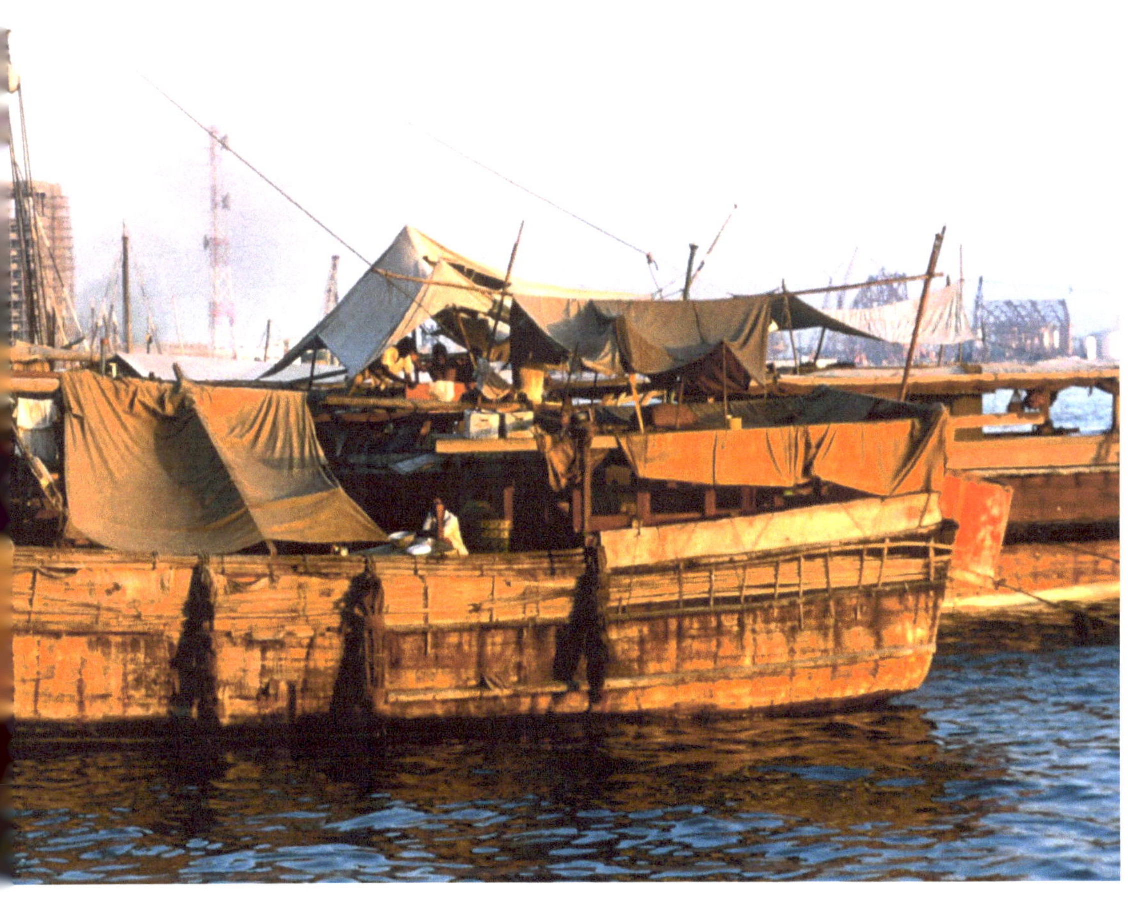

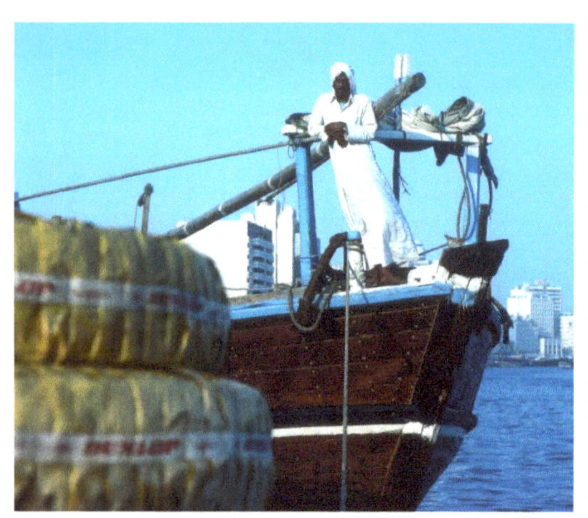
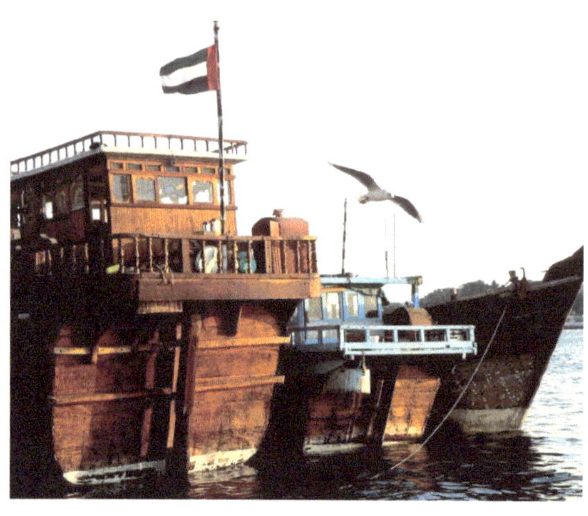

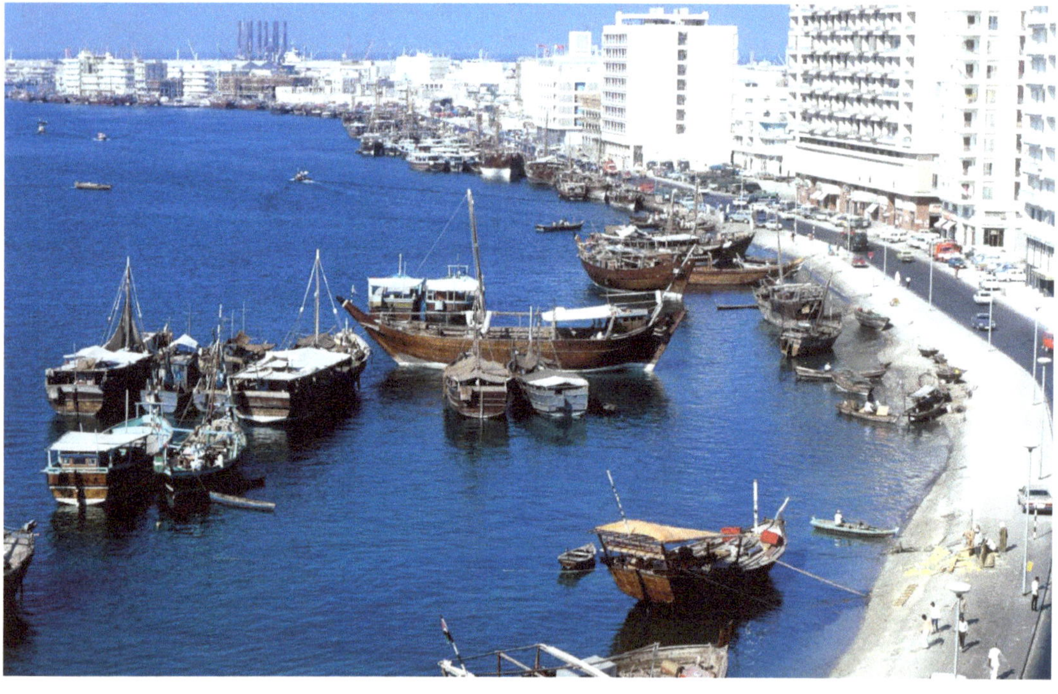

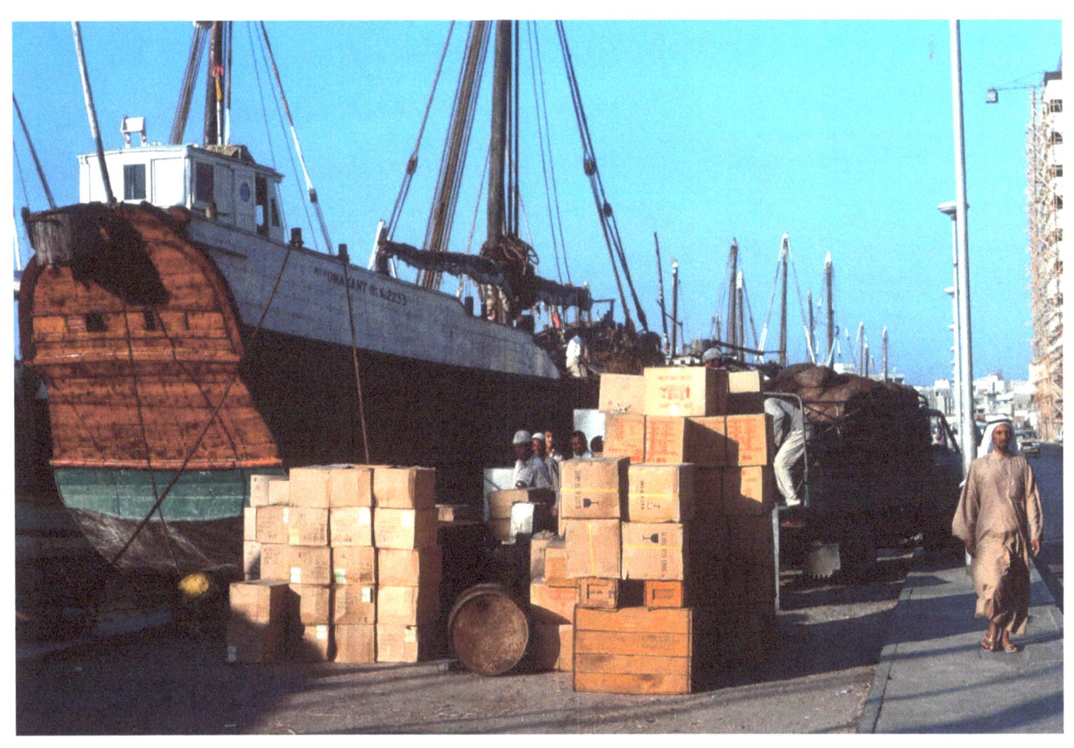

Dubai is synonymous with trade. The salt water creek winding through its commercial heart has provided a safe mooring for dhows since time immemorial. As many as 80-90 boats were once seen unloading cargo along the bank in Deira. Determined not to disrupt this historic activity, Dubai's former ruler, HH Sheikh Rashid bin Saeed al-Maktoum, ordered an underwater traffic tunnel to be built under the *khor*, as the creek is known in Arabic. Sheikh Rashid was the Vice President of the United Arab Emirates from 1971 until his demise in 1990.

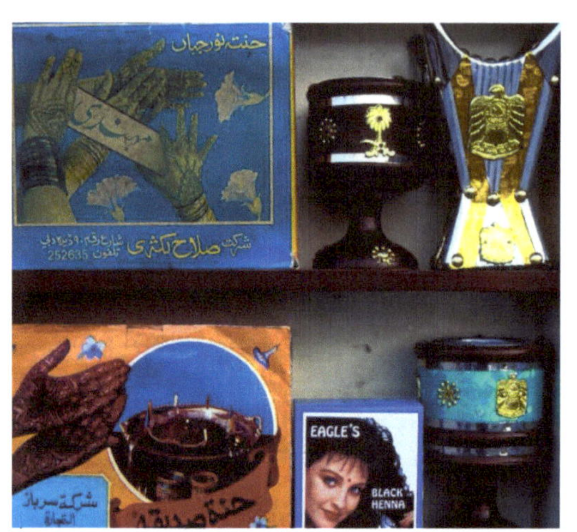

حنة نورجهان
شركة صلاح كشى شارع رقم ٩٠ ديرة دبي تلفون 252635
EAGLE'S
BLACK HENNA

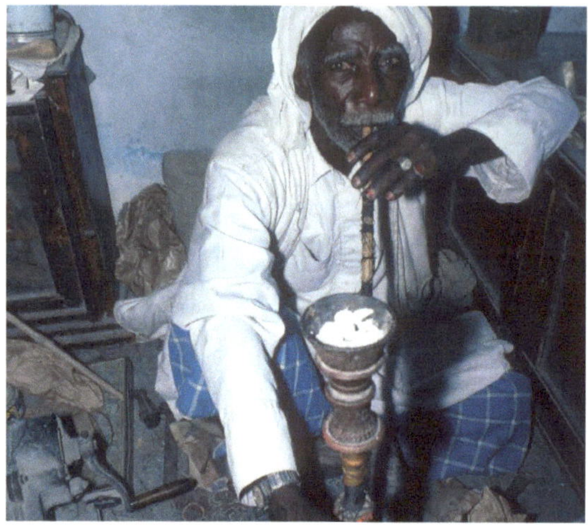

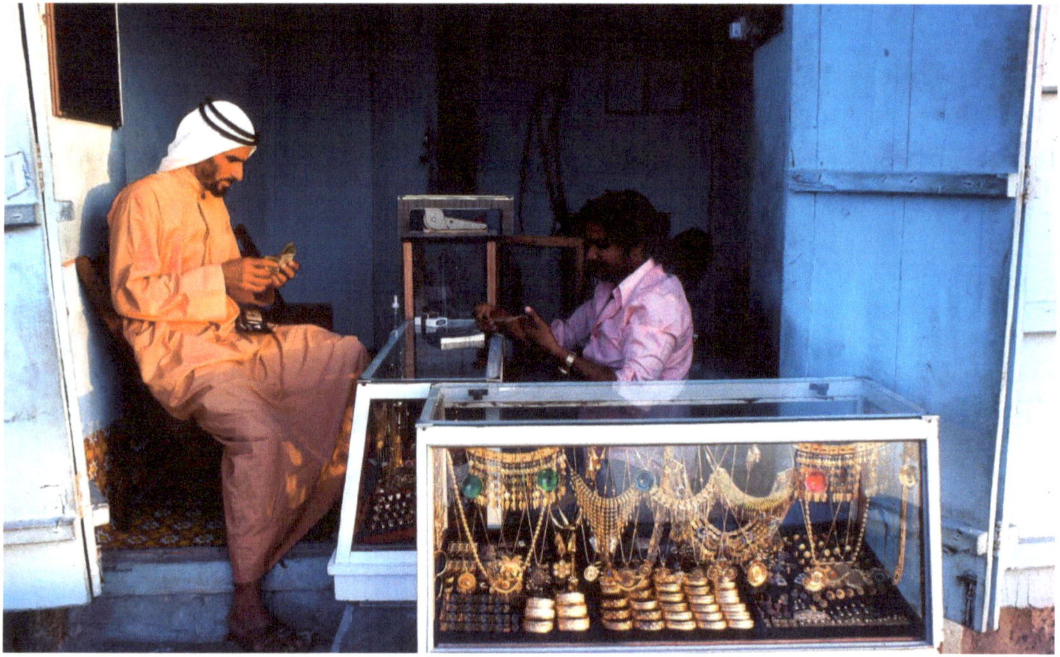

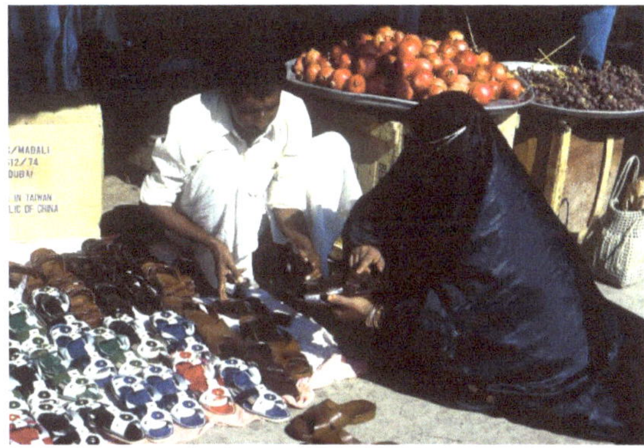

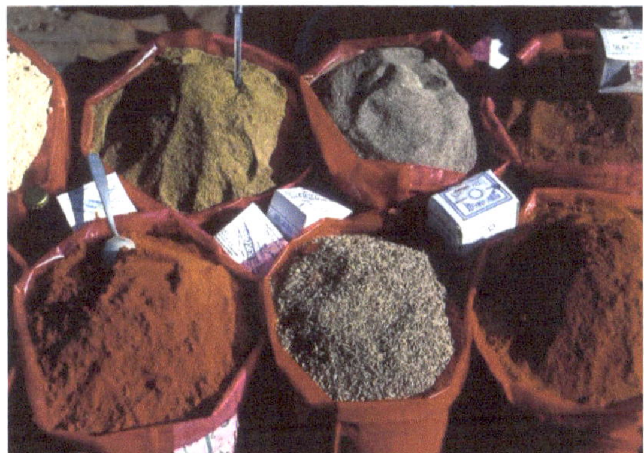

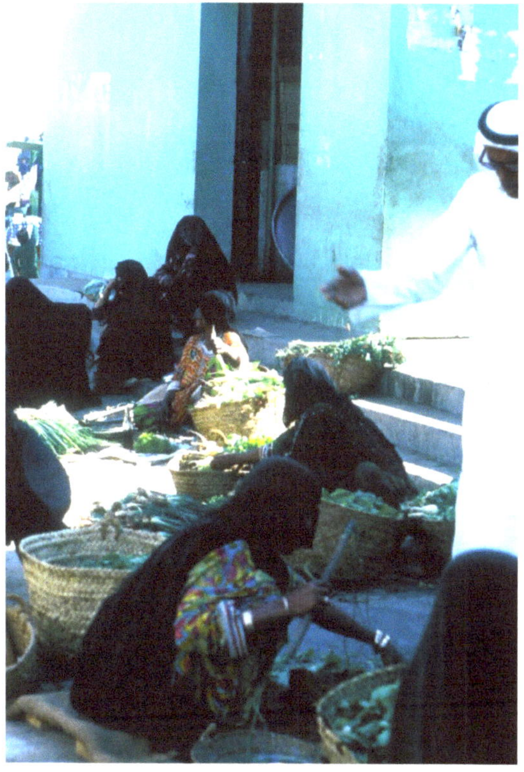

Souqs **or markets** were often located near a mosque so traders could easily attend Friday prayers. Not all traders were men however. Women in the open market in Dubai were the purveyors of vegetables. People shopped early for the freshest produce and to beat the heat. Air conditioned malls were still years away.

Opposite left to right: Arab women's beauty products Ajman; Trader in a tool shop Dubai; Gold shop in the old *souq* in Sharjah, 1974.

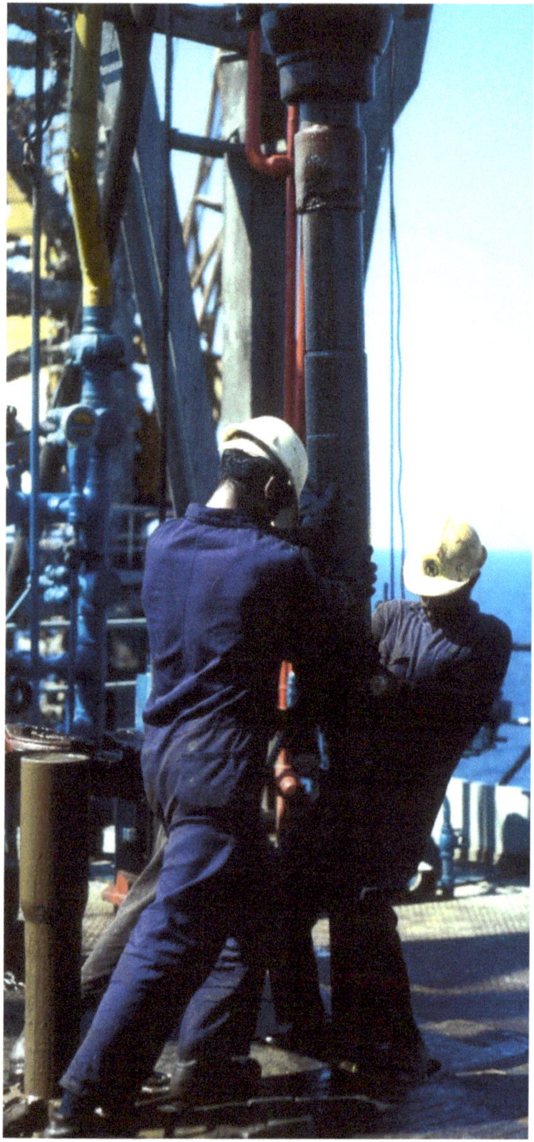

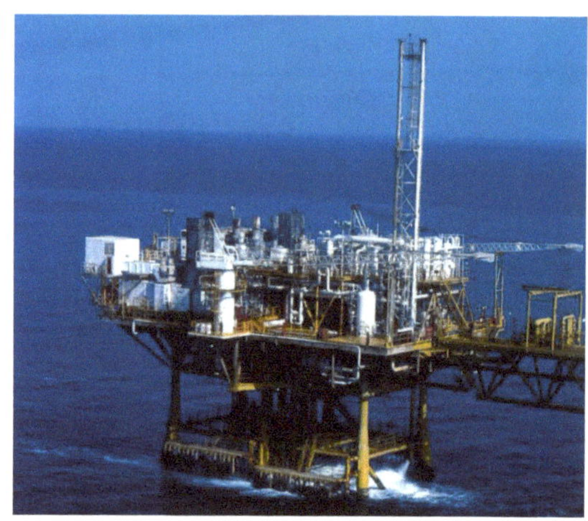

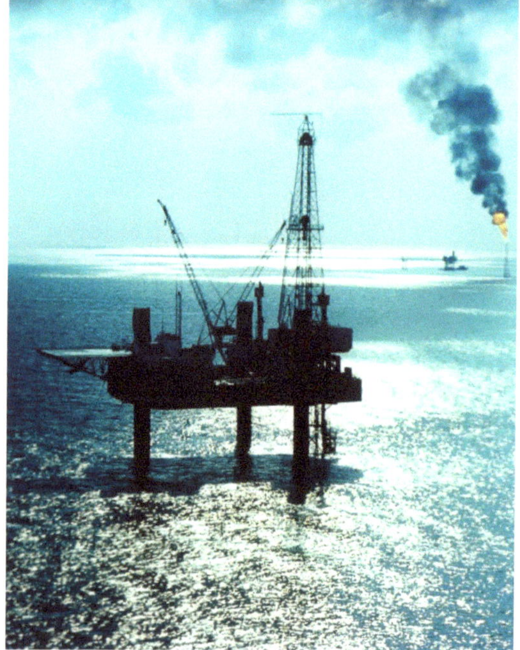

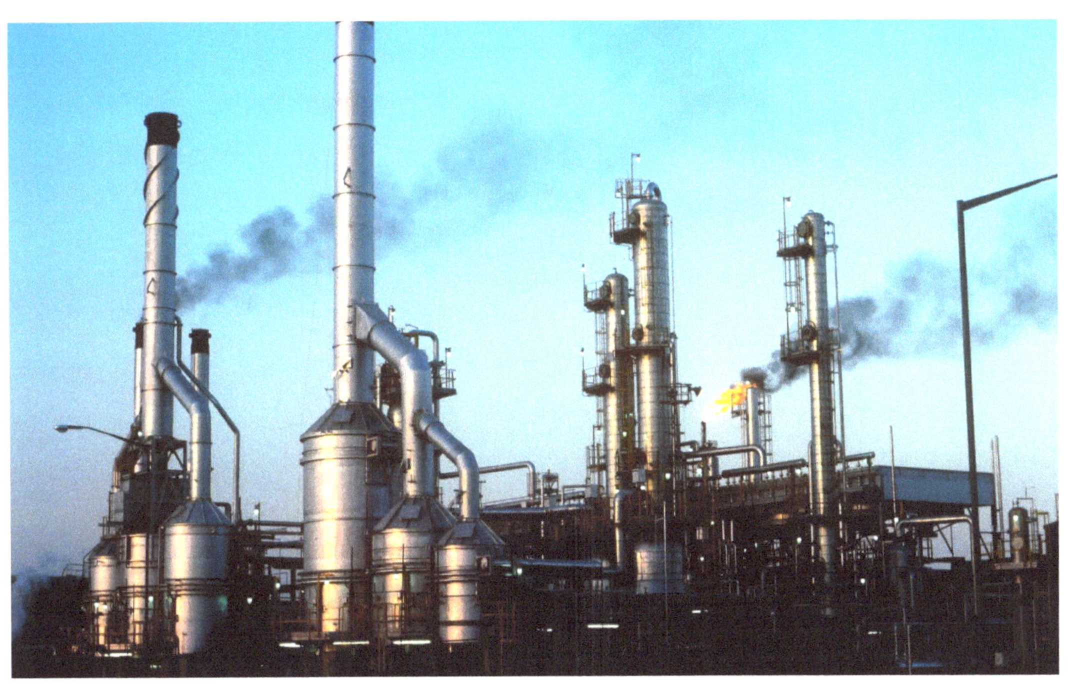

Nowhere in the world has the discovery of oil made such a dramatic difference to the lives of ordinary citizens as it has in the former Trucial States of the Gulf.

This page: the UAE's first oil refinery at Umm an-Nar island in Abu Dhabi opened in 1976 and produced at that time 15,000 bpd crude a day.

Opposite left: changing a drill head off Das Island owned by Abu Dhabi where the first oil exports were realised in 1962.

Opposite top: drilling for gas in Dubai's al-Fateh field, 1975.

Lower: oil-rig off Sharjah: commercial production began in 1974.

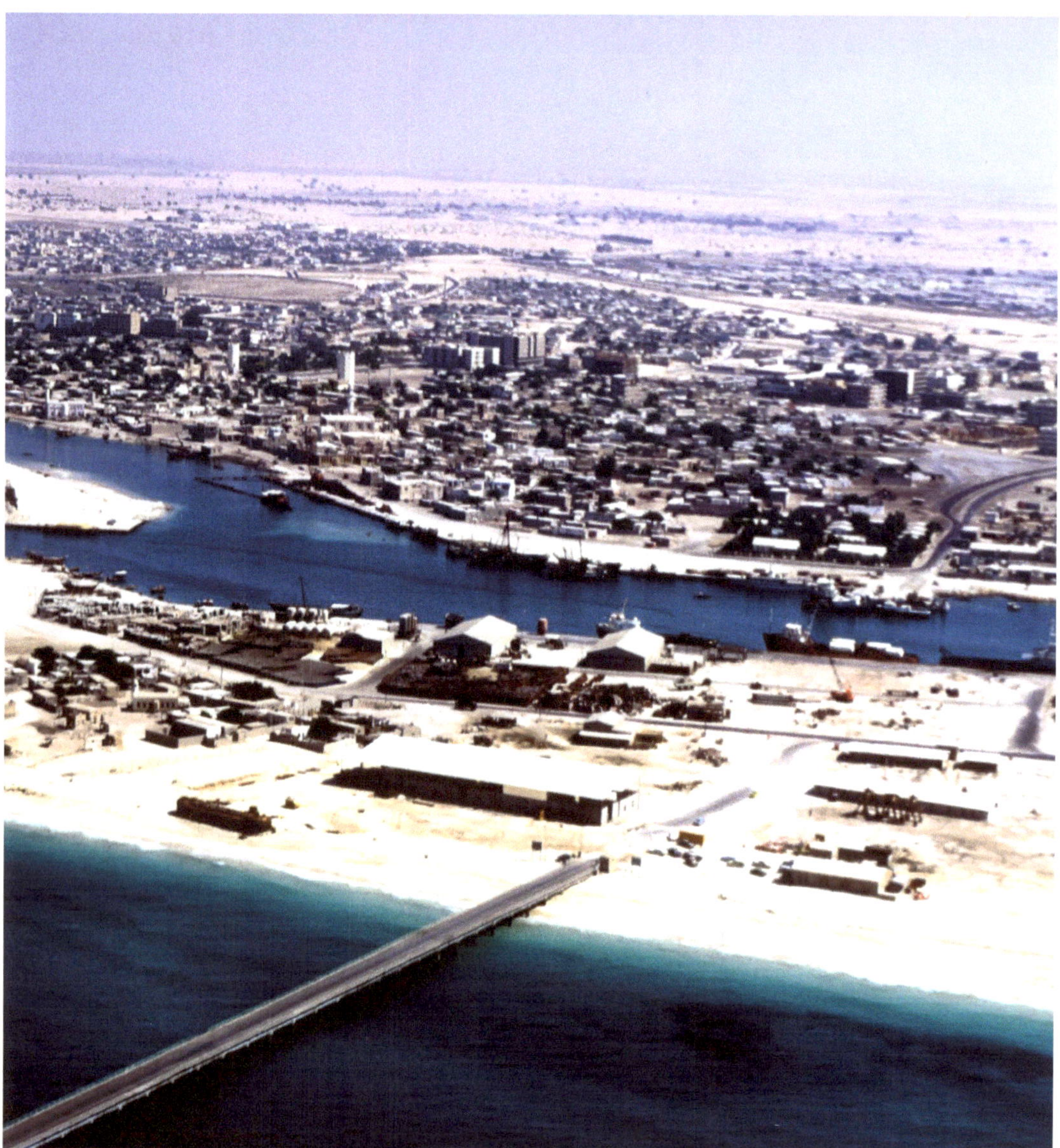

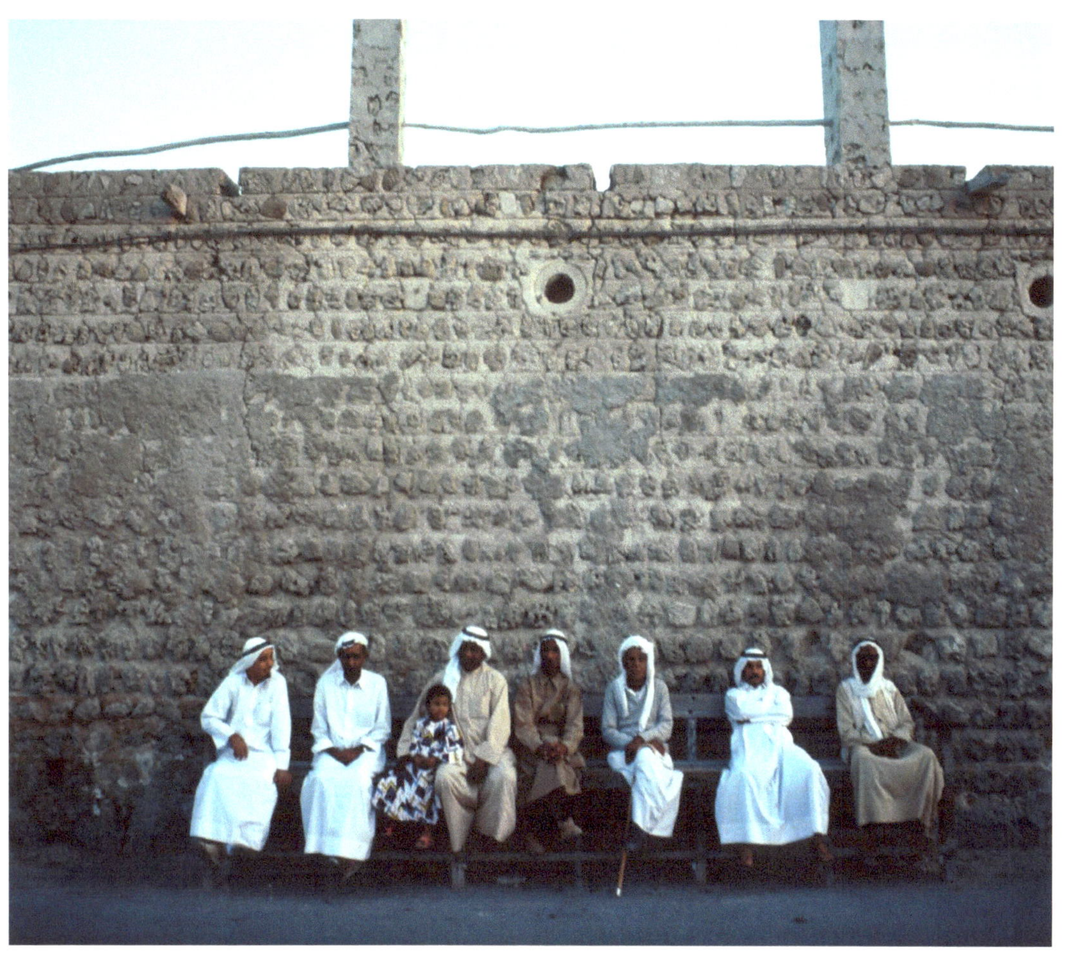

This page: citizens of Umm al-Qaiwain sit out the daylight hours of Ramadan, 1975.

Opposite: aerial view of Sharjah in 1975. The proximity of the desert is evident.

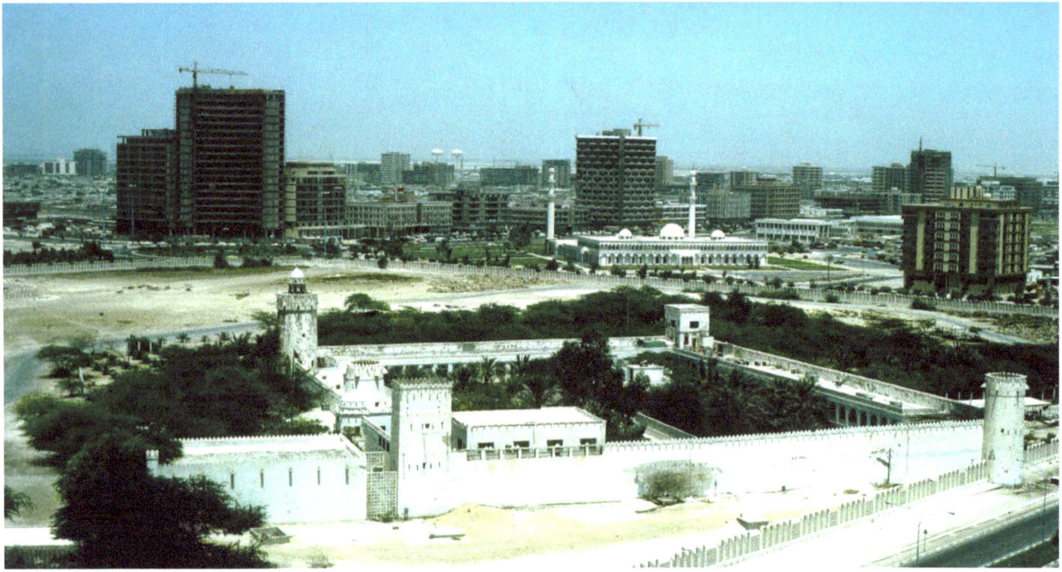

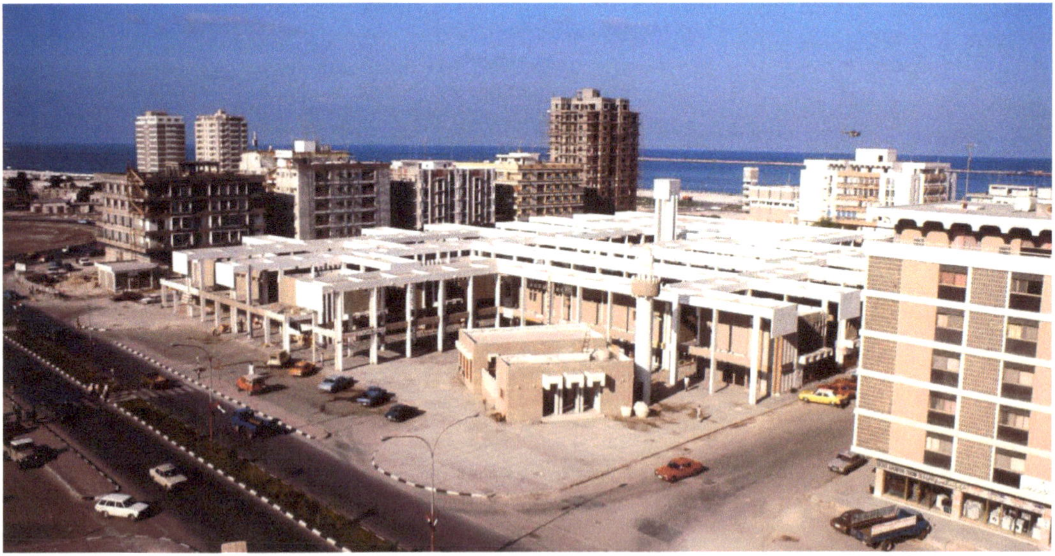

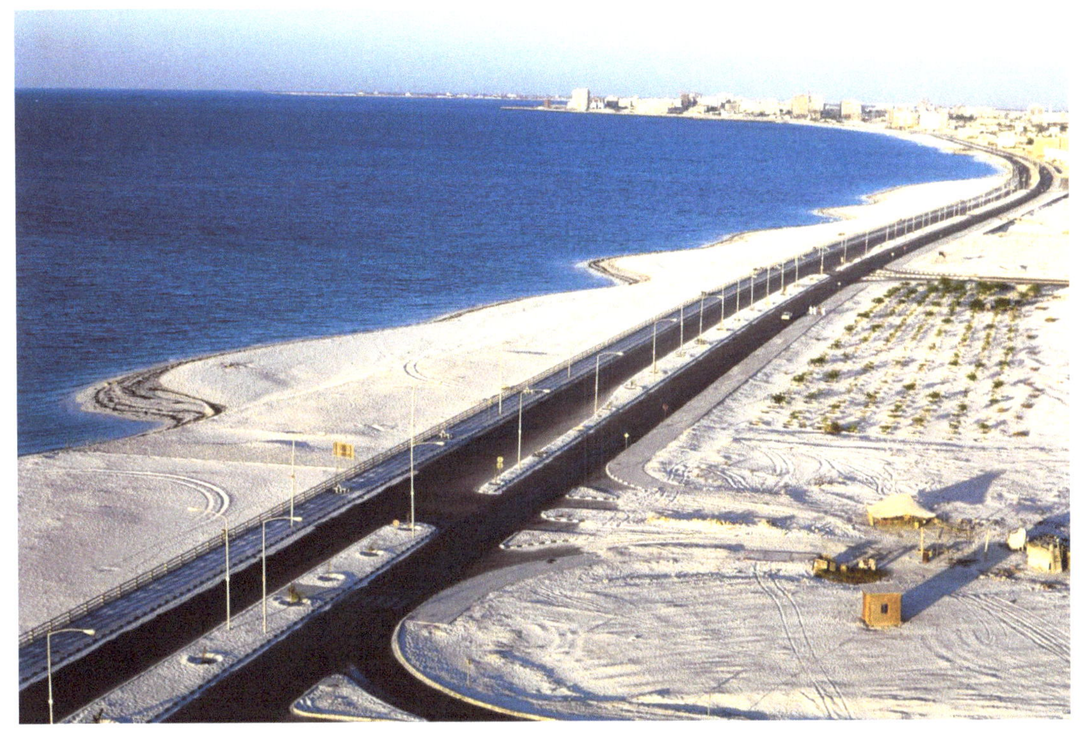

The start of development on Abu Dhabi island subsequent to the export of oil.

This page: the west coast before land reclamation schemes transformed it into the beautiful tree-lined corniche of today.

Opposite top: the ruler's fort, *Qasr al-Hosn,* built in 1761. It remained the only building on the island until the first oil revenues saw a boom in construction.

Opposite lower: view of central Abu Dhabi with the *souq* in 1977.

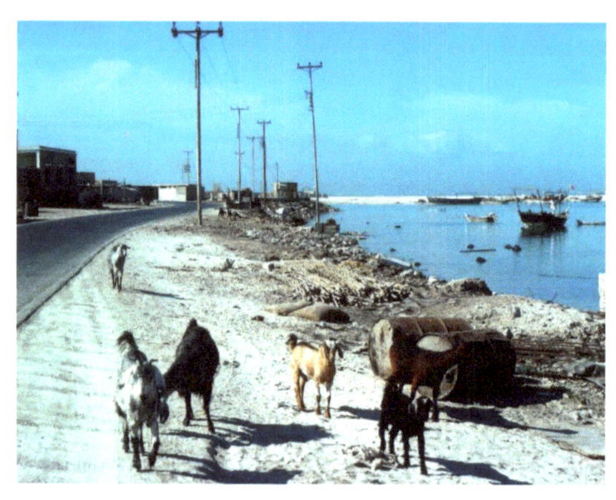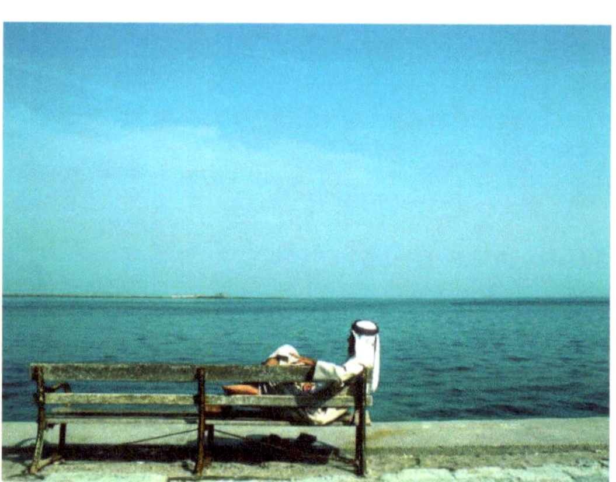

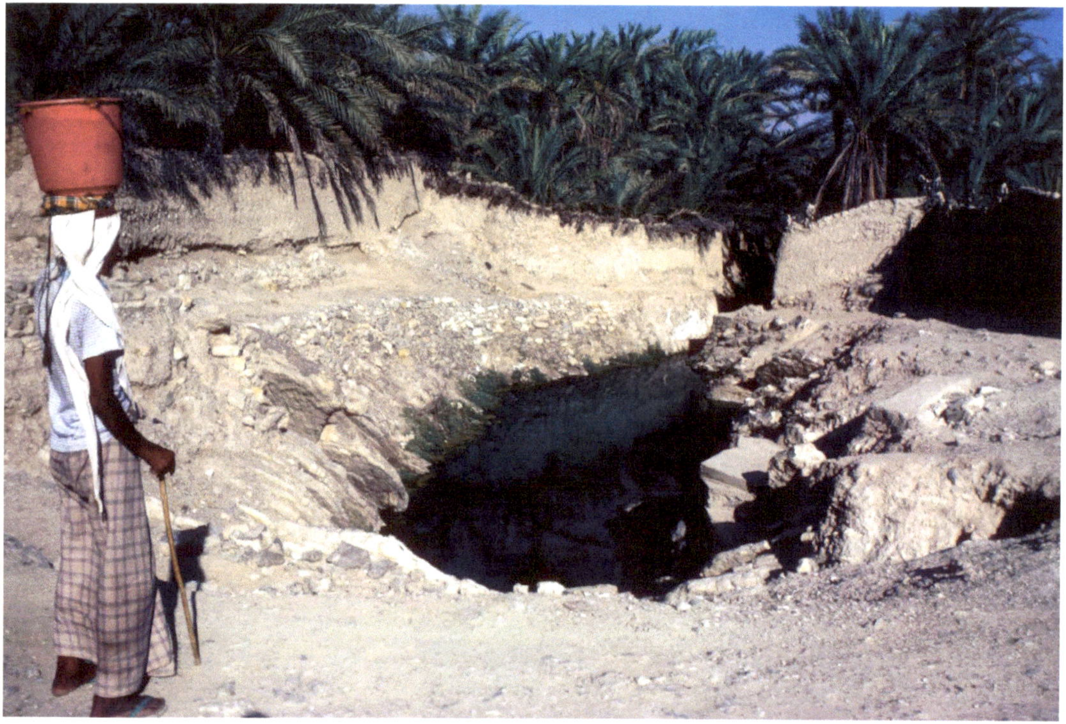

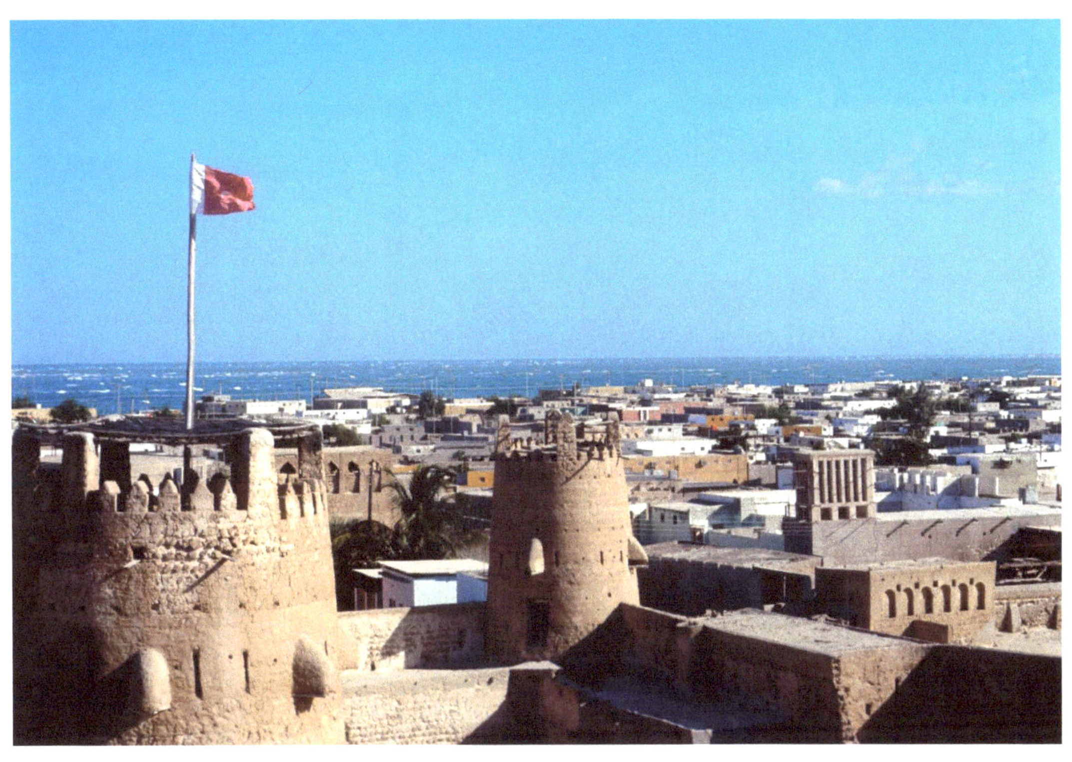

This page: the old town of Umm al-Qawain from al-Ali fort, built in 1775.

Opposite top left: the main street and dhow harbour in Ajman in 1974.

Opposite top right: seafront in the eastern emirate of Fujairah 1975.

Lower: the hot springs in Khatt, Ras al-Khaimah, 1975. Today a spa resort.

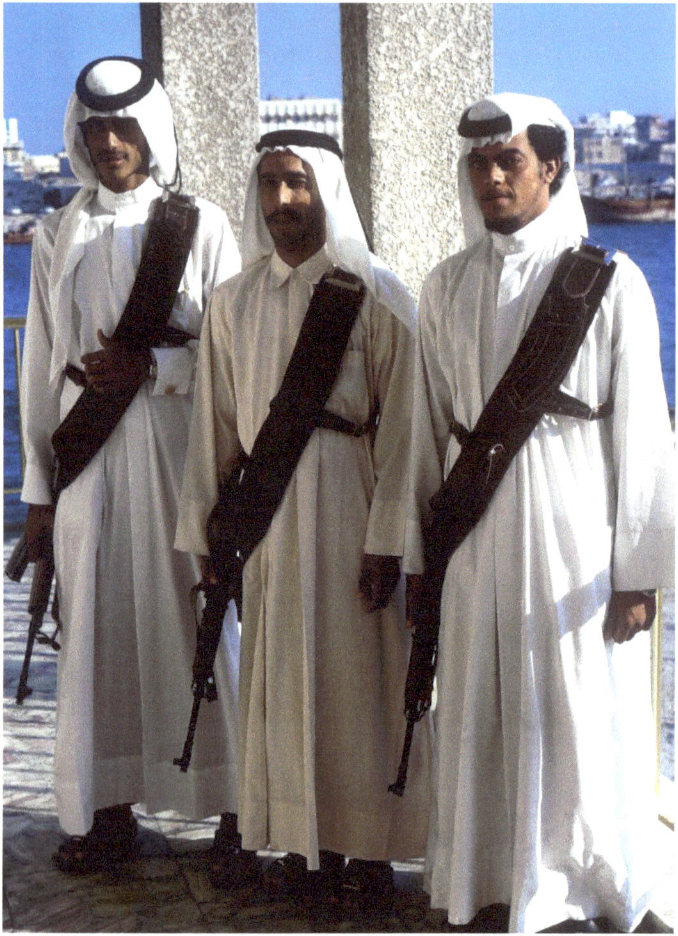

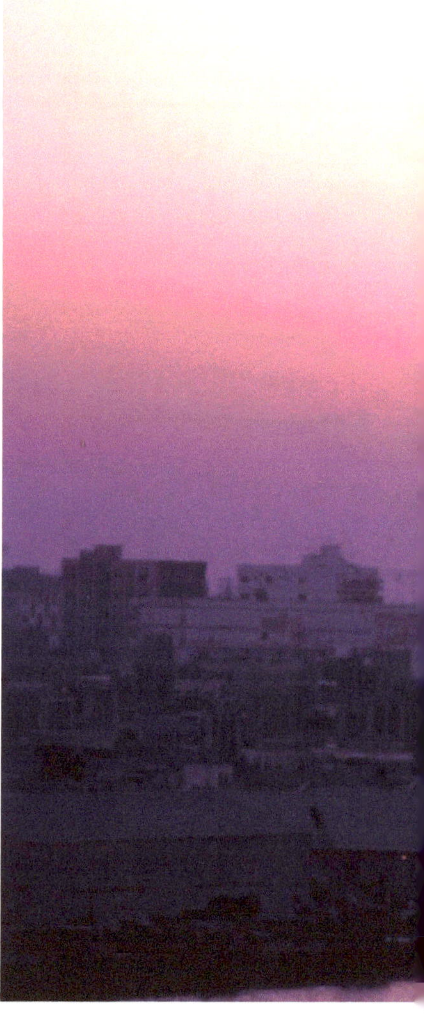

View of Burj Dubai with the ruler HH Sheikh
Rashid bin Saeed al-Maktoum's bodyguard, 1974

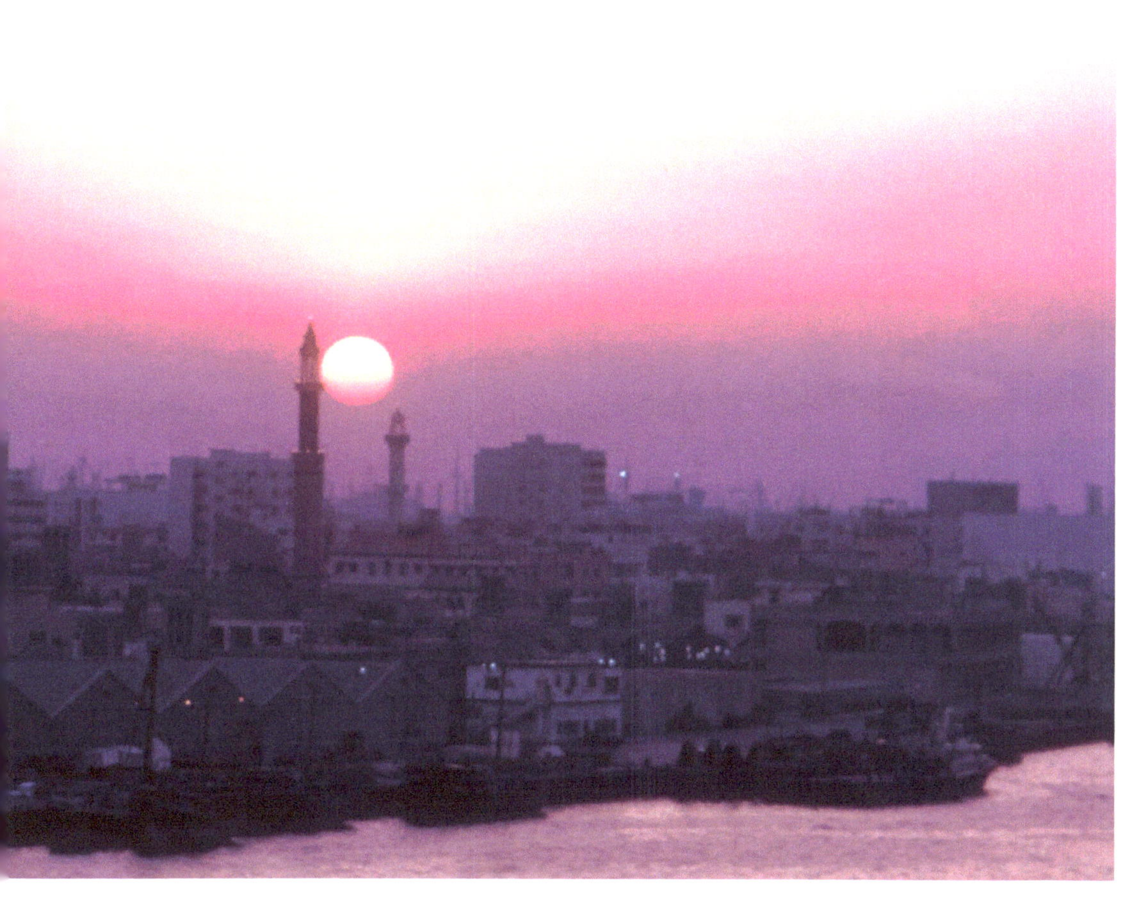

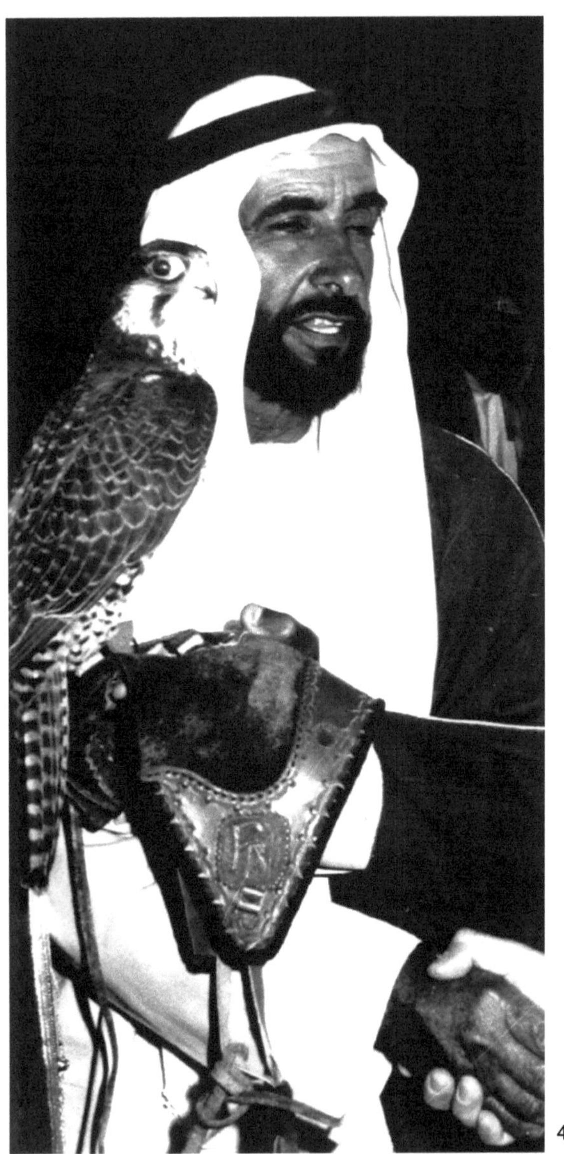

Sheikh Zayed is considered the founding father of the UAE whose vision shaped the nation into what it is today.

The former governor of the inland town of al-Ain, he replaced his brother, the Emir Sheikh Shakbut, in a bloodless coup in 1966.

A priority for Zayed was to set about building re-settlement homes for the Bedouin. But there were many priorities. The British had invested nothing in the Trucial States. and using his new oil wealth, Zayed constructed roads, hospitals, schools, literally everything needed to bring the UAE into the 20th century.

This page: HH Sheikh Zayed, 1976.

Opposite top: the Maqta Bridge linking Abu Dhabi to the mainland was built in 1967. Until then men and camels had to wade across at low tide.

Lower: Abu Samrah, one of the first towns built for the Bedouin, 1975.

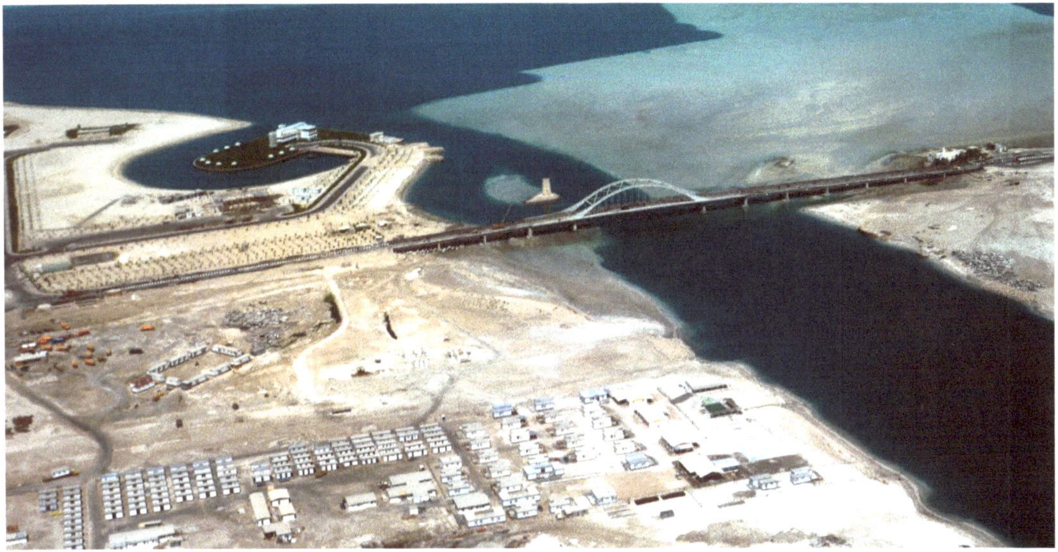

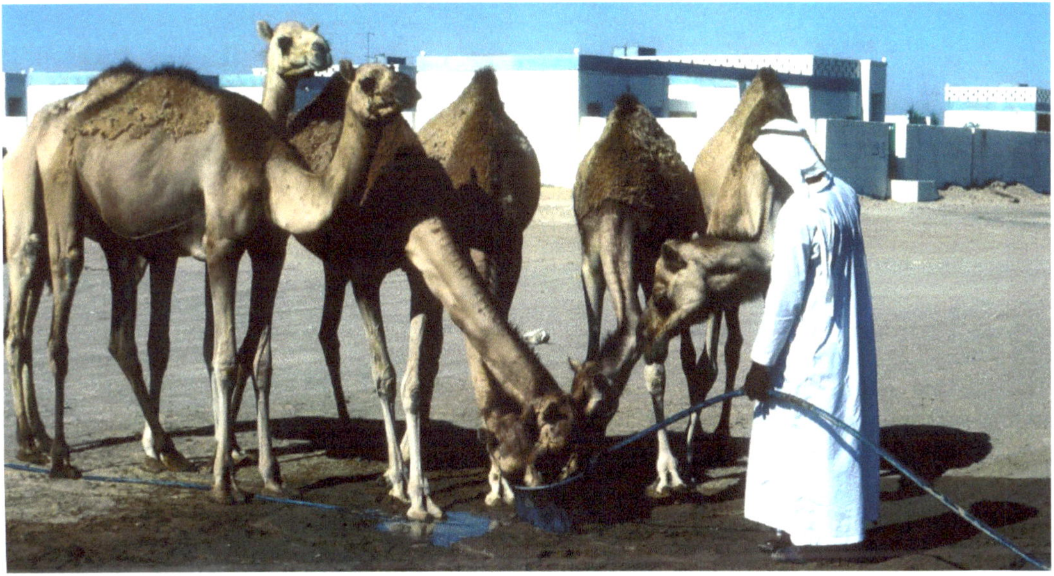

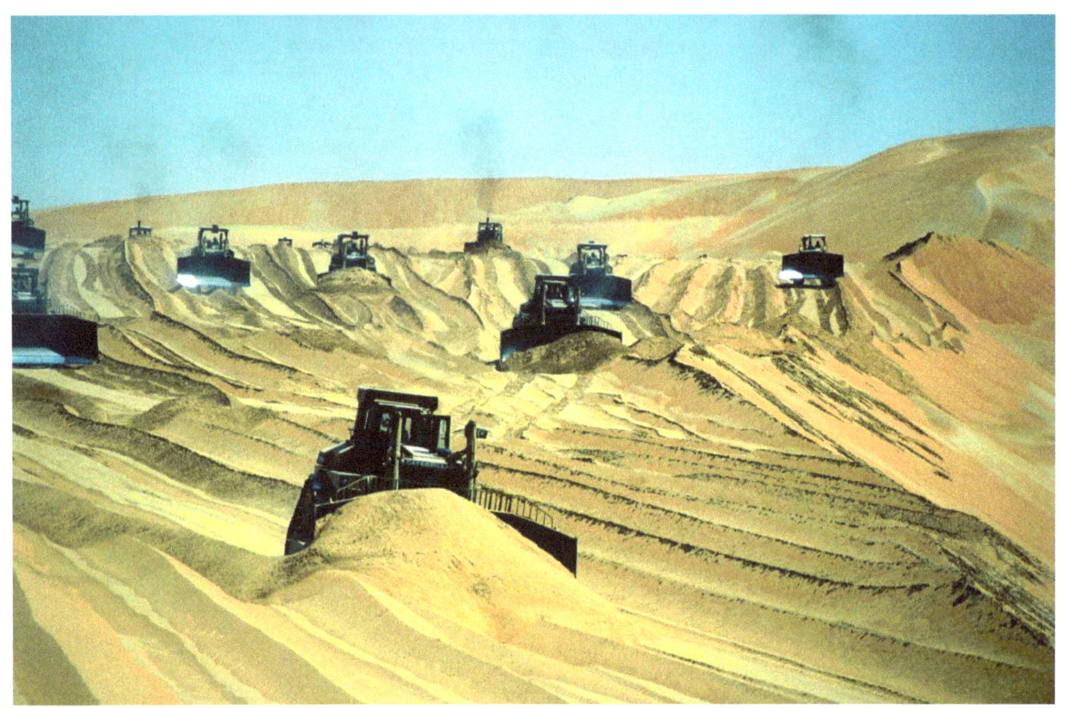

Archaeological evidence indicates the UAE was once a region of thick forests and abundant wildlife. And an avowed aim of Sheikh Zayed was to turn the deserts into productive farmland. Armies of bulldozers were brought in to level the dunes prior to the implementation of extensive afforestation schemes.

Opposite top: reclaimed desert sewn under pasture and protected from searing sand laden winds by dense tree cover. Dunes are seen in the distance.

Lower: tree planting on the Gulf island of Sir Bani Yas has since transformed it into a paradise for wildlife including the Arabian oryx and other vulnerable species such as the Arabian Tahr, desert gazelle and Barbary sheep.

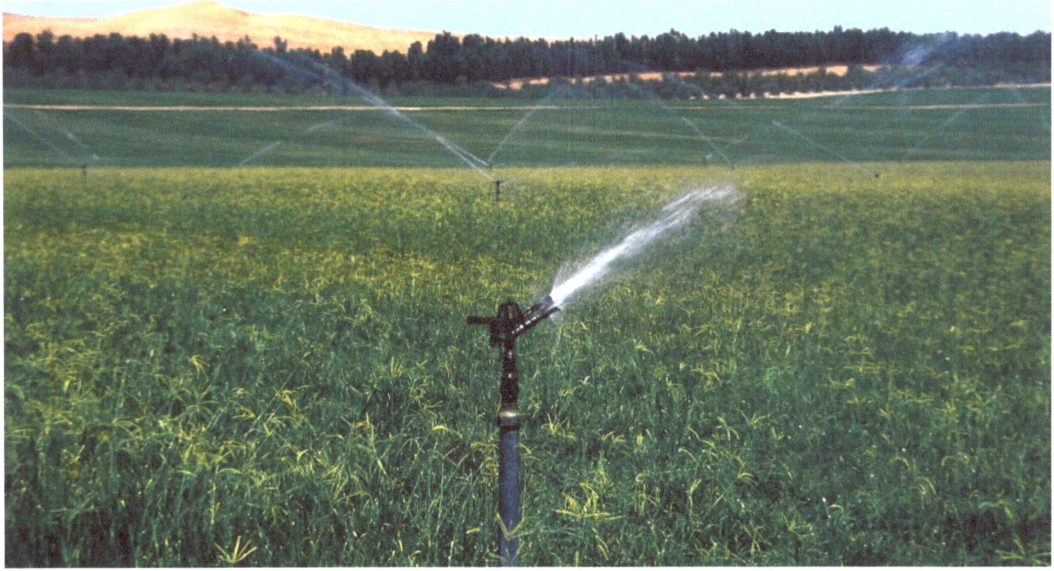

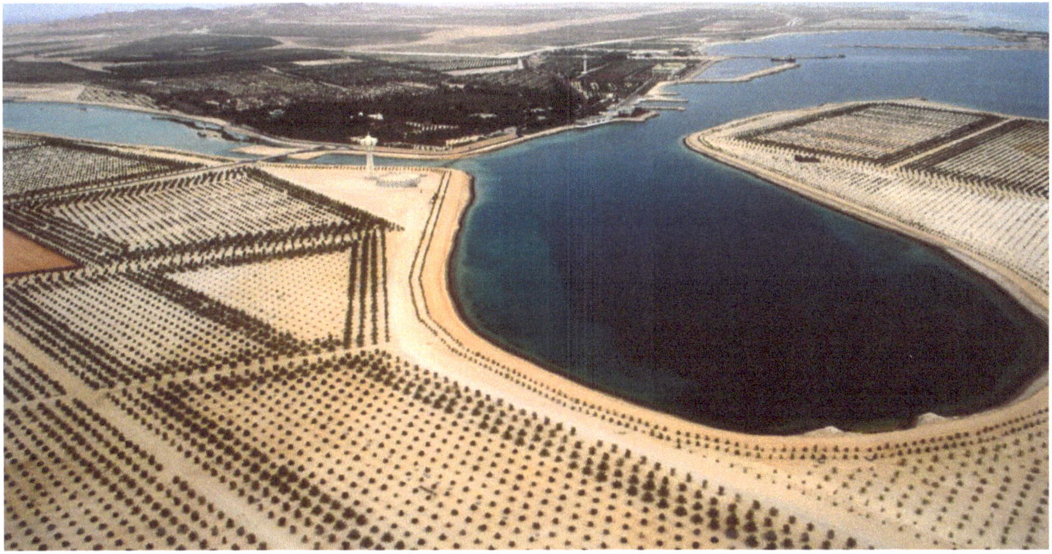

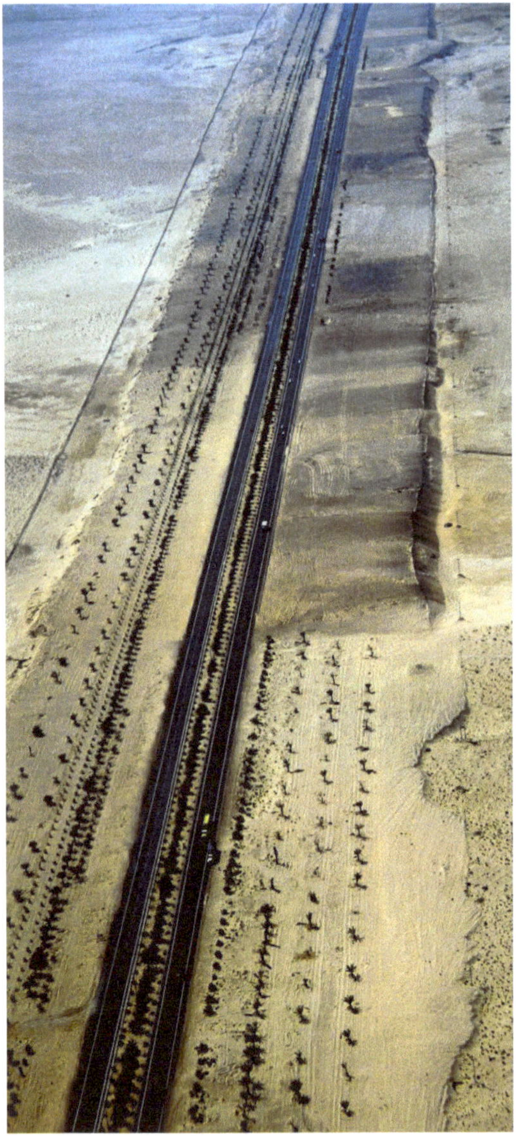

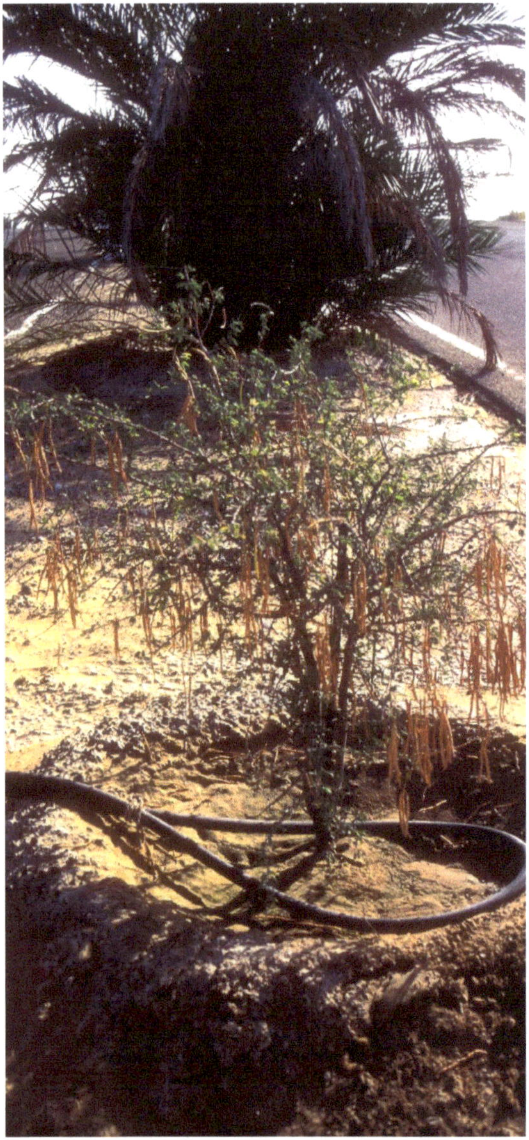

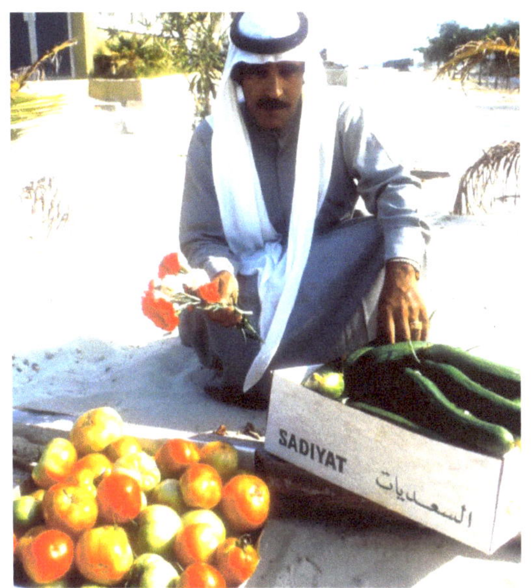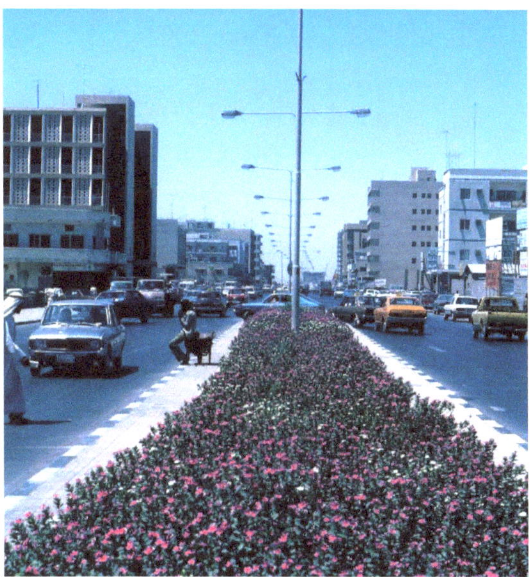

This page left: Sadiyat Island off the coast of Abu Dhabi was selected for early experiments in growing vegetables using hydroponic irrigation methods. Pictured is the first crop of tomatoes. Today the island is a cultural and leisure centre.

This page right: the first civic garden on the main road through Sharjah, 1974.

Opposite left: aerial of the road between Abu Dhabi and al-Ain in 1976. A tree-planting project started by Sheikh Zayed in the 1960s included more than a million trees. Each plant is sustained via an individual drip tap attached to more than 100 km of irrigation tubing. Abu Dhabi has won many international awards for afforestation programmes. Tree cover has also reduced summer temperatures by 1-2 degrees.

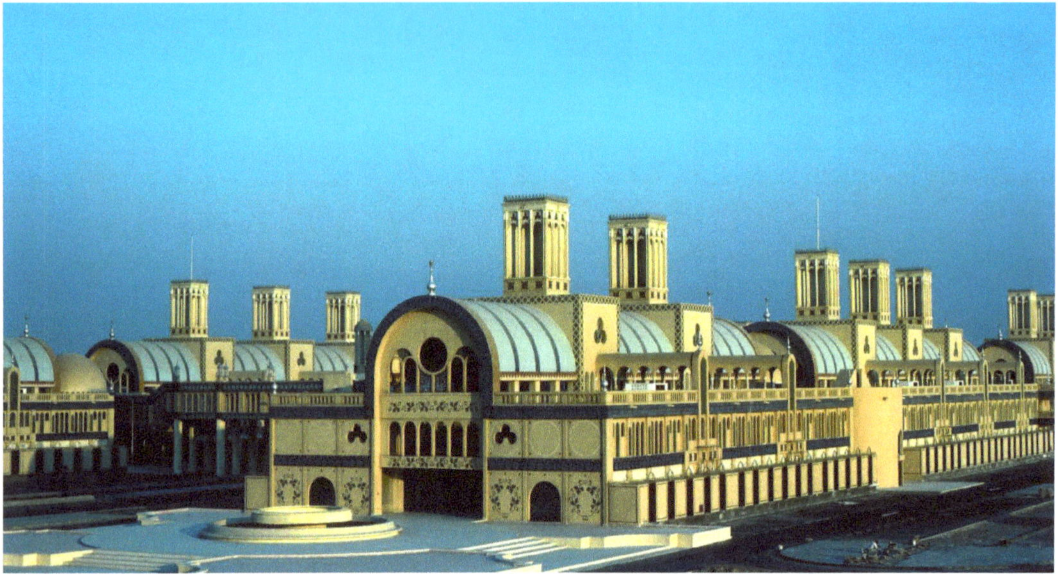

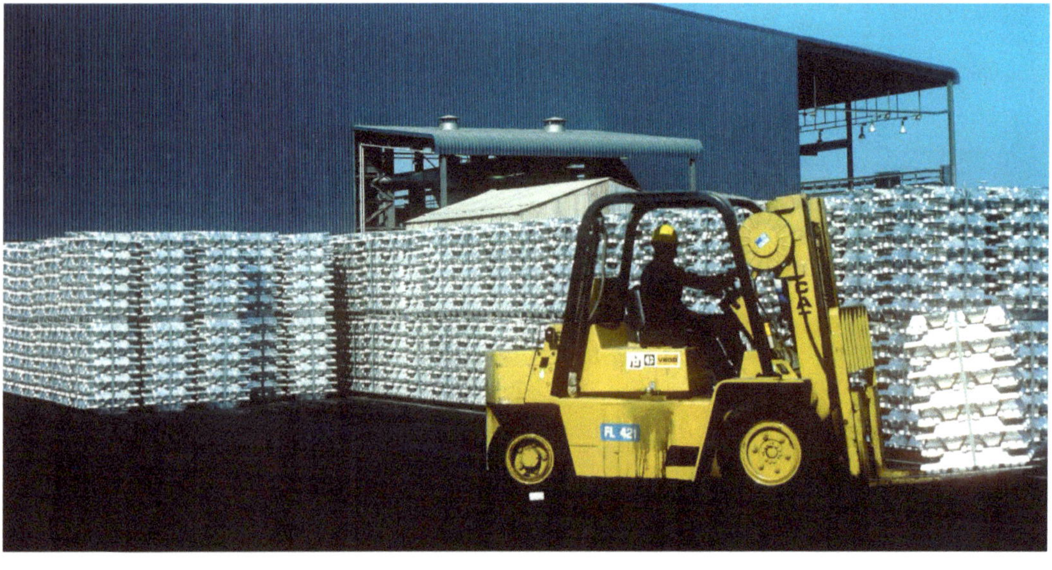

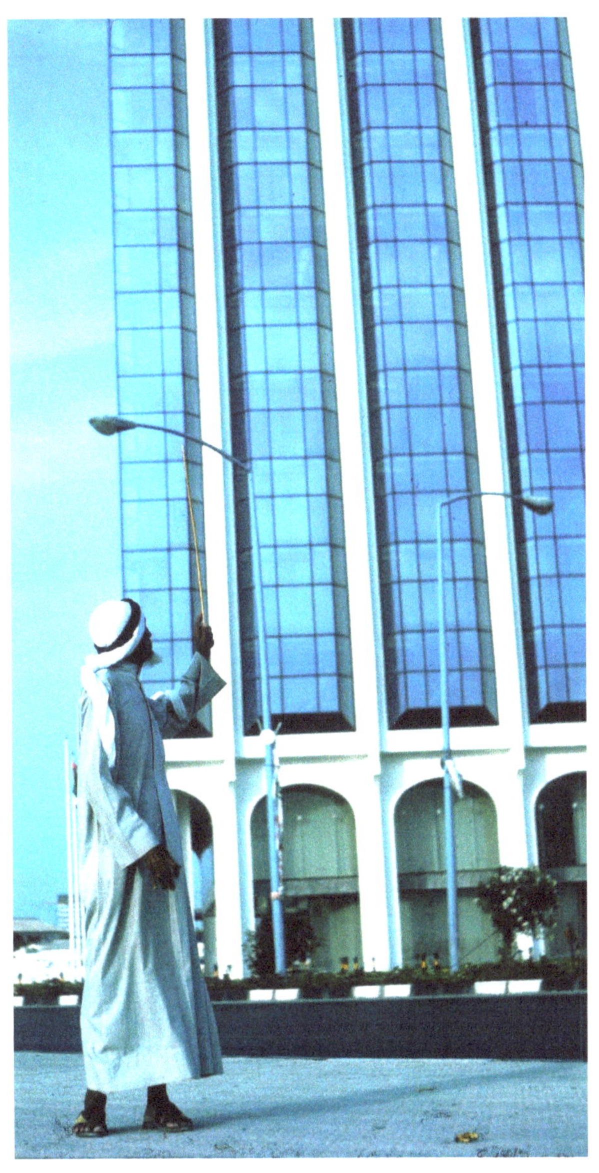

By the end of the 1970s, change was well underway in Abu Dhabi, Dubai and Sharjah and while the northern emirates lacked natural resources, the federal budget assisted with local projects such as clinics and schools.

This page: an old Bedouin admires the first highrise built in Abu Dhabi in 1976. The emirate now counts scores of skyscrapers over 180 m tall.

Opposite top: a 600 shop *souq* in Sharjah nears completion in 1978.

Lower: Dubai's big investment was an aluminium smelter opened by HM Queen Elizabeth II on her historic visit to the Arab States of the Gulf in 1979.

Following page: coastal scene in Umm al-Qawain, 1974.

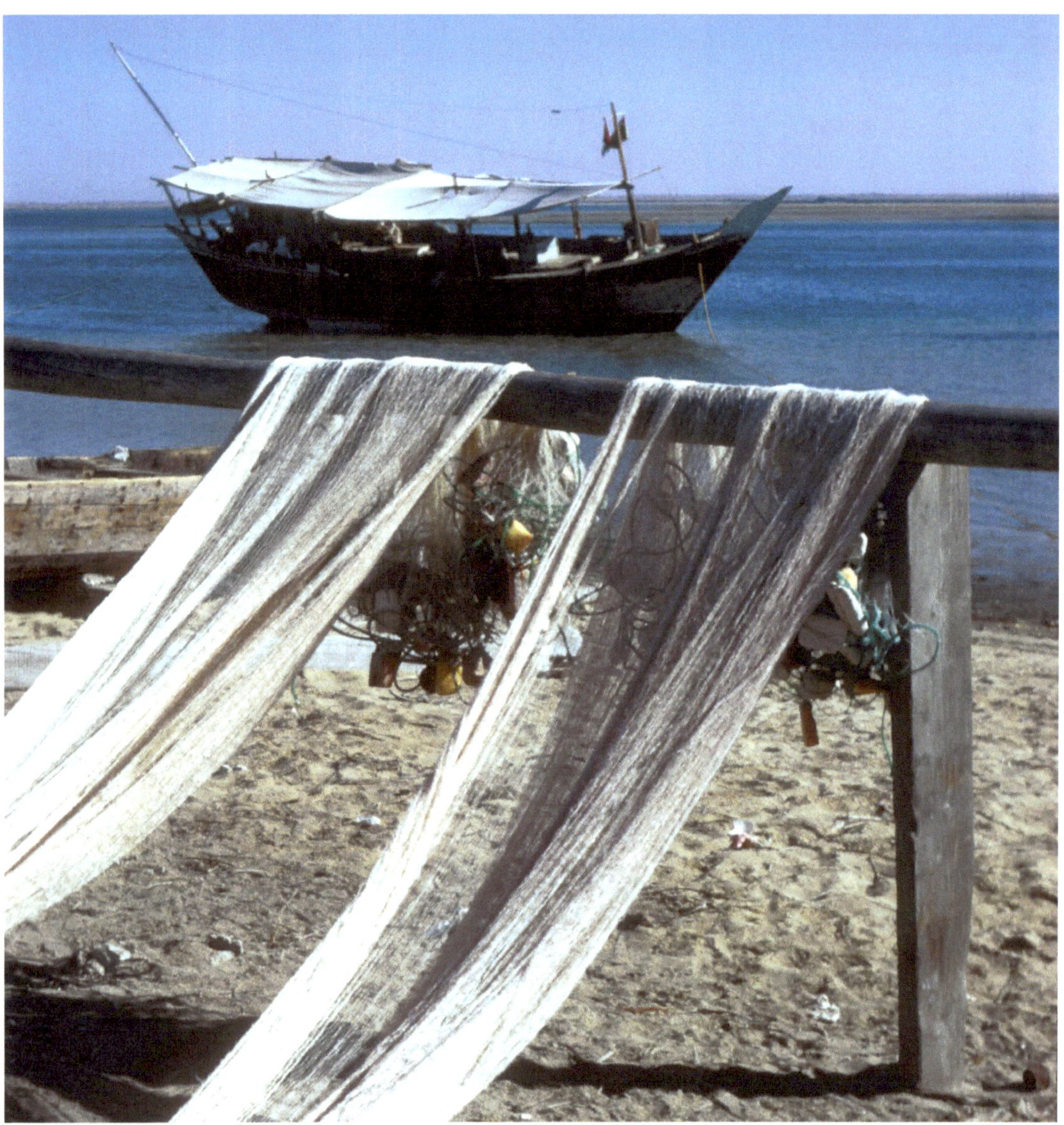